CHIEF JUSTICE JOHN MARSHALL

a reappraisal

A *bust* of *Chief Justice John Marshall by Felix W. de Weldon in the possession of the William and Mary Law School Association.*

CHIEF JUSTICE
JOHN MARSHALL
a reappraisal

Edited by W. MELVILLE JONES

Director, Marshall Bicentennial Program

College of William and Mary

PUBLISHED FOR

College of William and Mary

CORNELL UNIVERSITY PRESS

ITHACA, NEW YORK

PRINTED IN THE UNITED STATES OF AMERICA BY THE
VAIL-BALLOU PRESS, INC., BINGHAMTON, NEW YORK

Preface

THE contents of this book are largely composed of papers presented at a conference held at the College of William and Mary in Virginia on May 12 and 13, 1955. This conference was one of the events of the Marshall Bicentennial Program sponsored by the College of William and Mary, which began in September 1954 and concluded with the bicentennial month, September 1955.

A word or two concerning the organization of the conference may be informative. The sessions revolved around the general theme: "John Marshall: Two Hundred Years Later." The subject matter was divided into three parts: I, "Marshall and His Times," is discussed in Chapters Two, Three, and Four of this book; II, "The Power of Judicial Review," is represented by Chapters Five and Six; and III, "Some Special Contributions of Marshall to the Law," is the subject of Chapters Seven, Eight, Nine, and Ten. Professor

Preface

Swisher's able general introduction in Chapter One was written especially for this volume.

I am glad to extend my warm thanks to the many persons who so kindly aided in numerous ways in this undertaking. Among them I should like to mention Alvin Duke Chandler, President of the College of William and Mary, for his interest and constant encouragement; Dean Dudley W. Woodbridge and the members of the faculty of the Marshall-Wythe School of Law; Edward S. Corwin, Professor Emeritus of Jurisprudence at Princeton University, for his excellent suggestions and advice; William G. Harkins, Librarian of the College of William and Mary, and James A. Servies of the library staff for their valuable assistance with editorial problems; Mrs. Fraser Neiman of Williamsburg for her help with the Index. Above all, I express my special thanks to the contributors to this volume, both for the serious and scholarly effort which they gave to the preparation of the papers and for their splendid co-operation with the editorial work.

Acknowledgments are made to the following publishers who have kindly granted permission to quote from the books and articles indicated: Houghton Mifflin Company, *The Life of John Marshall,* by Albert J. Beveridge; G. P. Putnam's Sons, *Writings of James Madison,* ed. by Gaillard Hunt; Little, Brown & Company, *Speeches,* by Oliver Wendell Holmes; University of North Carolina Press, *The Commerce Clause,* by Felix Frankfurter; University of Michigan Press, *An Autobiographical Sketch of John Marshall,* ed. by John S. Adams; Harvard University Press, *Mr. Justice Miller and the Supreme Court,* by Charles Fairman; New York University Press, *The President, Office and Powers,* by Edward S. Corwin; University of Kansas Press,

Preface

A *Declaration of Legal Faith,* by Wiley B. Rutledge;
Louisiana State University Press, *The Judicial Power of
the United States,* by Robert J. Harris; *Harvard Law Review,* "The Retirement of Federal Judges," by Charles Fairman; New York Historical Society, letter from John Marshall to W. S. Cardell; Boston Public Library, letter from
John Marshall to C. F. Mercer.

W. MELVILLE JONES

*Williamsburg, Virginia
January 1956*

Foreword

BY CHIEF JUSTICE EARL WARREN

IT IS our pleasure to honor great men of another day, men who have contributed much to our national life and to the civilization of which it is a part.* We speak of them, of course, in gratitude, but we have another reason, even more personal to present-day Americans and in keeping with the necessities of our time. We meet here to strengthen our own convictions concerning government and law; to fortify our belief in a government of laws and not of men. We seek rededication to the cause of justice, between individuals, between citizens and their sovereign, and between the nations of the world. We reach for perfect justice, but we do not expect to grasp it, because history both profane and divine teaches us that as long as time and

* An address delivered at the Marshall-Wythe-Blackstone Ceremonies held at the College of William and Mary in Virginia, September 25, 1954.

human nature exist there will be issues to decide, causes to adjust. We learn from Holy Writ that even the angels quarreled and that Satan and his angels were banished to darkness for their wrongs. We know that the path of justice in every time and place has been rough, tortuous, and uphill. No nation has yet reached the summit. Exact justice has not been achieved. No mortal has embodied all its principles. We recognize, however, that civilizations of the past have advanced it; nations in all ages have made contributions to it, and individuals have either evolved or formulated or synthesized principles of justice in a way that has challenged the admiration and emulation of people in many lands—people who are interested in that kind of government which is premised upon freedom and the dignity of the individual. We honor those nations for their accomplishments and revere the memories of such individuals for their contributions.

As Americans, we are proud of our system of government and our standards of justice, although we claim neither originality nor perfection for them. We, too, have had our great men who have made contributions to the sum total of human knowledge in the field of justice. We do not deify them. Like the sages of other countries, they were people, subject to all the limitations of human beings. As a nation, we make no pretense except to a passion for justice based upon the dignity and rights of the individual. We stake everything we have on our belief that only through this kind of justice can there be order and contentment within nations and peace between the countries of the world. We believe this kind of justice is the rightful heritage of every human being and that it is his right and duty to achieve it.

Foreword

For three and a half centuries Americans, using the experience and wisdom of older countries from which we or our forebears came, have endeavored to develop in this section of the world a system of government and a body of law that will accord justice to everyone. We have made mistakes—many of them. People have at times succeeded in using our system for selfish and even oppressive ends. We have often been required to wipe some things from the slate and start again. At times we have been close to failure, but we have never failed in our climb toward the pinnacle of true justice. And we are climbing today to meet the test of Thomas Jefferson that "the most sacred of the duties of a government is to do equal and impartial justice to all its citizens."

We do not assume that justice is indigenous only to our soil or in our own people. Waves of passion, prejudice, and even hatreds have on occasions swept over us and almost engulfed us, as they have the people of other lands. In our efforts to guard against these things, we have called upon the wisdom of the ages. We have accepted unblushingly the contribution of those intellects of other nations and ages who, in accordance with the circumstances under which they lived, have placed foundation stones in the temple of justice.

Our own symbol of justice, the home of the Supreme Court of the United States, honors great nations of lawgivers. It is of Grecian architecture of the Corinthian order so loved by the Romans and used by them in a countless number of their public buildings. In the courtroom itself, we give public recognition to the lawgivers of all ages. On the frieze of one wall are the figures of ancients who made their contribution before the birth of Christ: Menes, Hammurabi, Moses, Solomon, Lycurgus, Solon, Draco, Confucius, and Octavian; and on the opposite wall the figures of those who came after Him: Justinian, Mohammed, Charlemagne, King John, St. Louis, Grotius, Blackstone, Marshall, and Napoleon. The most significant to us, of course, are the figures of those who expounded the two systems that are the most alike of any because premised on the affinity of lineage, language, concept, and emulation, the British and American. They stand side by side, William Blackstone and John Marshall. These men were contemporaries although not known personally to each other. The one had not been out of England; the other lived almost his entire life within a few miles of his beloved Virginia.

While Blackstone was writing his *Commentaries* on the law of England, Marshall was studying the great events of history upon which the rights of Englishmen were predicated in order to establish here a comparable system of justice. At that time, he and his compatriots were concerned not so much with a better system of justice than the English system as they were with having the same rights as Englishmen. A few years later he fought, along with Washington, at Monmouth, Brandywine, and Valley Forge to establish here a nation for that purpose. Blackstone expounded the law of England as it had developed by tradition, charter, statutes, and judicial interpretation for a thousand years. Marshall expounded our Constitution, a document of five thousand words, only a dozen years old, but which had been designed to establish for all times a more perfect Union of States that had but recently achieved their independence. That Constitution was an experiment in the science of government. Many people believed it to be a dangerous experiment. Many feared it and believed it would become another instrument of oppression. It was approved by the states only by the narrowest of margins. No one was certain if or how it would stand the test of time. One of the signers of the Constitution said, "Constitutions are not the same on paper as in real life." It fell to the lot of John Marshall to translate our Constitution from paper into real life, to enable it to meet the problems of a new, poor, war-tired, and divided country. To say that it took wisdom, foresight, patience, and courage to do this task is trite. But it is nonetheless true, and he did it for thirty-four years during the most formative and politically turbulent period of our national history, leaving at his death a greater imprint on our legal institutions than any American to this day has ever made. It is appropriate that this recognition should be given him in his beloved Virginia, where he lived all his life and in whose service he offered his life for the new nation he envisioned, in whose legislature he labored for the Constitutional Convention, where he worked for ratification of the Constitution, and which state he represented in the Congress. Born in the wilderness, he learned from his parents and from an occasional tutor, but largely from the life of his time and from the great men of Virginia in the causes for which men struggled in those days. What men he encountered in his native state!—Washington, Jefferson, Madison, Patrick Henry, Mason, Monroe, and a host of others immortal in United States history. Whether these men agreed in politics or not, they all had great minds, were passionately devoted to their own political philosophy, and each sharpened the minds of the others either through friendly intercourse or political contention. Marshall was the beneficiary of these associations as much as any American of those days, whether they stemmed from the adoration he had for his beloved chief, George Washington, or from his almost life-long political strife with his kinsman, Thomas Jefferson.

John Marshall has rightly been called the "expounder of the Constitution." The Constitution was new to the point of being without precedent when he became Chief Justice, January 6, 1801. The nation was poor as a result of years of warfare. Means of communication between the states were sadly lacking; there was no national economy; our standing among the nations of the world was deplorable; the states were divided in interests and politics; men held passionate views concerning the relationships between the three branches of government and between the federal and state governments. The leaders were men of powerful intellect and passionate convictions. There were those who would center most power in the federal government. There were those who would leave practically all power in the states. It was Marshall's mission in life to pursue a course somewhere between those two extreme positions, through the construction of the new Constitution, in a myriad of cases that arose during his thirty-four years as Chief Justice. He had spent a horrible winter at Valley Forge with Washington, and the weakness of the government under the Articles of Confederation had seared his soul. He believed in a strong central government—federal supremacy in all matters within the domain of the federal government. He believed that the Constitution should be construed liberally to accomplish that end, and he confirmed the power of Congress to do so in these historic words: "Let the end be legitimate, let it be within the scope of the Constitution, and all means which are appropriate, which are plainly adapted to that end, which are not prohibited but consist with the letter and spirit of the Constitution, are constitutional."

He believed that if we were to remain a nation we must have a national economy, and that any strong economy must be based upon the scrupulous performance of contracts and the orderly regulation by the central government of commerce among the states and with other nations. He realized that if we were to command the respect of the world, we must meticulously fulfill our international obligations and honor the treaties we make. All of these desired results he achieved through decision after decision until they became embedded in our law.

But perhaps the greatest contribution he made to our system of jurisprudence was the establishment of an independent judiciary through the principle of judicial review. In a case instituted the first year of his incumbency, he rooted this fundamental principle in American constitutional law as our original contribution to the science of law.

This and many other of his decisions aroused a storm of protest as being beyond the words and intent of the Constitution, but for thirty-four years in accordance with his belief, stone by stone, he built the foundation of our constitutional structure, and he constructed it sufficiently strong to support everything we have since built upon it. In those thirty-four years of his incumbency, he wrote 519 of the 1,106 opinions handed down by his Court.

He did not go with the tide of public opinion or the course of politics. Often his opinions were contrary to both, but he continued to build, patiently, logically, courageously. His sense of duty is epitomized at the time of the trial of Aaron Burr, which he conducted fearlessly in spite of the intense feeling of the public and the national administration against the defendant. In the conduct of that case, as a circuit justice, he said: "That this court dares not usurp power is most true. That this court dares not shrink from its duty is not less true. No man is desirous of becoming the peculiar subject of calumny. No man, might he let the bitter cup pass from him without self reproach, would drain it to the bottom." And he did his duty in that case, unpopular though it was.

He lived with this conviction throughout his long career. When his work was done and he passed away in Philadelphia on July 6, 1835, in the eightieth year of his life and the thirty-fifth of his chief justiceship, he was acclaimed by friend and foe alike as a man of virtue and great accomplishment.

His long-time friend and illustrious associate, Joseph Story, said of him: "Chief Justice Marshall was the growth of a century. Providence grants such men to the human family only on great occasions to accomplish its own great end. Such men are found only when our need is the greatest. His proudest epitaph may be written in a line—'Here lies the expounder of the Constitution.'"

The people of Philadelphia accorded him a hero's farewell, and as his body was borne along the streets to the dock for transmittal to his beloved Virginia, the Liberty Bell tolled from the belfry of Independence Hall. Then a strange thing happened. A great cleft appeared in the side of the bell, and like Marshall's voice, it too became still forever. It was taken down and placed in the Hall. It remains there today for all to see—the symbol of our liberty—while the memory of John Marshall abides with all of us as that of "the great Chief Justice" and "the expounder of our Constitution."

CHIEF JUSTICE JOHN MARSHALL

a reappraisal

I. Introduction

BY CARL BRENT SWISHER

CITIZENS of every succeeding generation do honor to themselves by honoring the statesmen of the past. The year 1955, marking the two-hundredth anniversary of the birth of John Marshall, provided occasion for thoughtful memorials to the memory of the greatest of American Chief Justices. Since he was a member of the parade of distinguished Virginians produced by his state during his period, and since it was at Virginia's College of William and Mary that his limited experience at higher education was obtained, it is most fitting that this college should be the place of presentation of the testimonials and appraisals incorporated in this book. The several chapters, delivered as lectures on May 12 and 13, 1955, fall into a pattern with three major divisions. The first division presents Marshall in relation to the political and professional life of his times and the impact of his thinking as measured

by criteria of the present day. The second division deals
with Marshall's major contribution in the field of judicial
review. The third division deals with his special contributions to the law. The purpose of the paragraphs which follow is to highlight these major divisions for illumination
of the contributions of the individual authors.

I

Whatever the period in history that concerns us at the
moment, when we think about the Supreme Court we
tend to do so in terms of present problems and present
points of view, and even of present personnel. We think of
a Court which only a quarter of a century ago was sharply
divided over the scope of protection to be given to rights
of property, of the victory of New Deal ideology, of the
liberal-conservative conflict in appraisal of the work of
the Court, and of the extent of involvement of present or
recent justices in the political issues of the day. Since Chief
Justice Marshall made his contribution to our constitutional system during the first third of the nineteenth century and not in the middle portion of the twentieth, and
since, unlike Chief Justice Warren, he had a tradition to
build rather than a tradition to adhere to or to break, it
is hard to see the former Chief Justice in the light of the
latter. So it is that for an understanding of Chief Justice
Marshall we have to go back to the conditions of his
times, to the personnel, to the needs, to the points of view
that then prevailed. We have to remind ourselves, among
other things, as is done in the first lecture herein, that the
statesmen of the Revolution were for the most part not
revolutionaries in the social and economic sense of present-

day thought, but were merely separatists from Great Britain who were more interested in stability and economic betterment along traditional lines than in novel ideas of social justice. They did not intend to permit the success of their Revolution to give birth to still other revolutions of which they might not approve.

Yet it is hard to classify Marshall and his contemporaries in terms of the liberal-conservative categories of the present day or of twenty-five years ago. The term "liberal," as noted in the second lecture, has currently been stretched to impossible thinness in attempts to make it cover all things desirable, and a reaction has developed a cult of the "new conservatism" to perform somewhat the same function. Marshall can be appraised not by pinning either label on him but only by determining what it was that he sought to conserve and what he sought to set free. Having seen the feebleness of such central government as existed under the Articles of Confederation, he showed little interest in writing into the new Constitution protections against a government that needed vast additions to its strength if it was to give stability to business. He sought protection for business at a time when the great body of property was in the form of land, when liquid capital was scarce, and when there was virtually no employee group which needed protection against employers and owners and which had the political power to enforce it. Present-day issues involving the control of liquid capital, the regulation of industry, and the protection of labor and the community generally against powerful corporations were issues hardly conceived of in Marshall's time. We have to measure him by his handling of the problems of his own day, and not of ours.

Chief Justice John Marshall

Even in the conception of the judicial task itself we need to remember that attitudes and ideas have vastly changed, or at any rate have taken on important modifying facets since the early 1800's. With significant but usually brief intervals of disillusionment, we have had more than a century wherein to entrench Marshall's belief in the sanctity of the Constitution, his injunction that in constitutional matters the Court should never forget that it was a Constitution that it was expounding, and his emphasis on the fact that ours is a government of laws and not of men. One of the longest and most important periods of disillusionment has been that beginning with the era of the 1920's and Justices "Holmes, Brandeis and Stone dissenting." Beginning also, oddly enough, about the time of the publication of Albert J. Beveridge's monumental *Life of John Marshall,* lawyers and laymen alike have engaged in intensive analysis of judicial motivations and interests. They have examined social, economic, and political backgrounds and affiliations and interests to determine the source of judicial decisions. Much has been done to disillusion the public about the alleged nonpolitical character of Supreme Court decisions and to demonstrate the biases and frailties of the men wearing judicial robes.

Here again, as in our third lecture, we need to re-examine the performance of Chief Justice Marshall in terms of current methods of analysis if the similarities and dissimilarities between his period and ours are not to appear different from what they actually are. Any position taken by a judge in constitutional matters is likely to appear "political" if there is a great deal of opposition to it. On the other hand, to few of us does a position seem "political" if it has behind it our own sentiments and the sentiments

4

of the people whom we most respect. Seen from this point of view, Marshall's nationalism, for which he is so much lauded, and even his insistence that the realities of political action be concealed behind the doctrine of "a government of laws and not of men," can be classified as in some sense "political." Here again, as in connection with characterizations as "liberal" or "conservative," it is necessary to go behind the "political" label to discover what it was in essence that Marshall stood for and what were his methods of making his convictions effective. Here, as always, we need to free ourselves from "the tyranny of labels."

II

In any treatment of the career of Chief Justice Marshall his entrenchment of the doctrine of judicial review stands central. Although he did not originate the doctrine, he did establish its effectiveness, once and for all, for the American judicial system. The several speakers in this series do not challenge the fact that Marshall's official assertion of the doctrine, in *Marbury* v. *Madison*, was encased in the then-current furies of partisan politics and, some of them think, in the politics of a rather low order for judicial participation. But they do find in the action of the Court a high measure of judicial statesmanship. The interpretation thereafter made of the doctrine is the important consideration. It can be carried to the extreme which one lecturer notes in his challenge to the phrase "judicial supremacy," another label that requires careful examination. The judiciary is not supreme in the sense that it is solely responsible for measuring legislative and administrative action against the Constitution. The legislative and executive branches also have that responsibility, and they exercise it constantly. They deal with innumerable problems of constitutionality that the judiciary cannot reach unless and until they become involved in litigation. Furthermore, there are constitutional problems which the judiciary itself classifies as "political" and which because of that classification it refuses to touch, leaving the "political" branches with full responsibility. Only in a limited sense, therefore, is the judiciary "supreme."

Even so, and in spite of the fact that in the half-century immediately following the decision in *Marbury* v. *Madison* not a single act of Congress was found by the Supreme Court to be unconstitutional, Marshall's opinion in that case drove home to the people the fact that in most important constitutional areas the Supreme Court would have the final say, if cases were appropriately brought before it. The Constitution was demonstrated to be "higher law," and the judiciary as the final and in some sense a "higher" interpreter. Furthermore, however "political" the opinion may have sounded to Jeffersonians who were castigated by it, it had an elevation of tone that down through succeeding years has continued to lend dignity to the constitutional document and to the judiciary as its prime interpreter.

Marshall brought to the Supreme Court a sense both of dignity and direction. Under three preceding Chief Justices it had faltered and demonstrated unsureness and lack of vision as to its function. Neither Jay nor Rutledge nor Ellsworth succeeded in imparting the tone which Marshall's leadership quickly gave. None of them showed his clarity of thought with respect to the powers of the national government and the relations of that government to the states. If the explanation lay in the fact that the three of them served but briefly and that one had to withdraw for want of Senate confirmation, it nevertheless remains true that two of them resigned their judicial positions instead of remaining to see what could be made of the Court they headed, and that one of them, John Jay, declined an opportunity to return to the Court, leaving the chief justiceship to be filled by Marshall. Marshall, by contrast, demonstrated all the vigor of action and clarity of purpose that could safely be displayed at a time when the other branches of the government were manned by his political enemies. Instead of withdrawing because of the inevitable frustrations of his position, he remained in office until his death in 1835, a period of service longer than that of any person ever appointed to the Court except Justice Stephen J. Field. In that third of a century he led in making the Supreme Court essentially what it has been ever since.

Clear assertion of the doctrine of the superiority of the Constitution over federal statutes and of the power of the judiciary to strike down federal statutes which it deemed in conflict with the Constitution established an attitude in support of many later decisions striking down state measures. Exercise of this power, although having precedents before Marshall became Chief Justice, required all the persuasiveness that could be brought to the task in the face of the resistance of jealous state governments and Jeffersonian critics. Although in some instances Marshall resorted to the low level of anonymous publication to answer his severe critics, his official opinions retained the loftiness that characterized his performance generally and set the tone of American constitutional law.

As the lectures demonstrate, he was concerned with developing the power conferred upon the federal government and with restraining the states from encroachments on the federal area and upon property rights protected by the Constitution. He was not primarily concerned with the personal and civil rights which the Constitution also protected. That area belonged to the Jeffersonians and to the judiciary of later years.

III

The third group of lectures presents some of Marshall's special contributions to law. Here, in connection with the controversy over the place of the common law in our constitutional system, Marshall is portrayed as a political economist, as a craftsman in the development of the commerce clause, and as the leader of an ever-changing group of justices in the development of our constitutional pattern.

The illusion is here dispelled that Marshall was relatively unlearned in the law of the past. He could cite cases amply when he deemed citation relevant. But the relevance of the common law to the law of the Constitution was a matter of prolonged controversy during the early years, and for the most part Marshall preferred to argue legal questions in terms of constitutional principles. Those principles (bearing the flavor of natural law) were often illustrated by decisions in English common law, but for Marshall they did not derive their potency from these cases. As a result of developments in the Marshall period it is at once true that "there is no common law of the United States" and that the common law has been enormously influential in determining the character of federal law. This complicated subject is here studied with care.

As always, the Supreme Court during the Marshall period was deeply involved in the economic problems of the day. This means, not that the justices were profoundly learned in economic theory, but rather that the impact of the law was primarily on economic events. In accordance with natural-law philosophy, Marshall assumed the right of men to engage in business, to own property, to make contracts, and so on. For him a major purpose of the newly established federal government was to assure stability to property, protecting it not only against individual marauders but also against the states. As spokesman for the Court, he interpreted the contract clause to prohibit state impairment of contracts even when made by the states themselves. Far more important, he erected the charters of private corporations into contracts which the states could not impair, thereby paving the way for the dominance of corporate enterprise in our society and so forestalling primary development of business enterprise at the hands of government. Utilizing the doctrine of implied powers, he upheld the establishment of a national bank and set a precedent for the expansion of federal powers, not that we might have a federally dominated socialistic regime but that property and the right to do business might be protected against governmental interference.

Of the decisions of the Marshall Court in the economic field, the most important may have been those interpreting the scope of the commerce clause. From the commerce power, along with taxing and war powers, comes the vast regulatory and proprietary power of the federal government over enterprise today. Marshall chose to see the commerce clause in the large and to shield the federal power against state encroachments via concurrent commerce power, police power, or other concepts. True, he did not finally assert the exclusiveness of the federal power, and he left the subject in a confusion which harassed the Taney Court and the Court of even later periods, but he did protect the right of the federal government to regulate where it saw fit—paving the way, indeed, for ultimate exercise of power which might have amazed and horrified him. In this area the credit or the blame, as the case may be, must be shared by later generations.

Until recent years it has been the custom to speak of Chief Justice Marshall as if he, standing alone except for a bit of help from Justice Story, had constituted the Supreme Court during his period and as if the other members of the Court were nonentities and without influence. Closer examination is showing this not to be true. It is, of course, true that he spoke for the Court in most of the important cases and that he discouraged the writing of dissenting and concurring opinions. He sought to have the Court speak impersonally as a Court rather than as individuals or aggregations of individuals. In so doing he built up the conception of the Court as an impartial instrument of the law, as an impersonal instrument of "a government of laws and not of men." Yet it was neither by coercion nor craftiness that Marshall secured a high degree of unanimity and anonymity among the justices. His chief justiceship was characterized by the kind of leadership that neither maneuvered nor coerced so much as it promoted the flexible development of a common body of constititional convictions among the men who worked with him. The working of the Court under his leadership represented co-operation at its best. There was disagreement, it is true. Some of it, particularly through the pen of Justice William Johnson, who tried valiantly to maintain not merely the reality but also the show of independence, found expression in the *United States Reports*. But to a high degree the preliminaries of judicial thinking and disagreement were concealed from the public when official opinions were written. The opinions represented the best syntheses of corporate opinion that could be attained.

Subsequent generations have been the beneficiaries of the Marshall conception of the judicial function. For all the criticism of personal and professional enemies, Marshall built for the American people a Supreme Court the prestige of which has never been completely undermined and which, when damaged during critical periods, has been eventually restored. The constitutional doctrines sponsored by his Court have been further developed, modified, or delimited as conditions and sentiments changed, but no sharp break with them has ever been necessary. Under tremendous strain the Court faltered for a period, it is true, lacking that firm body of supporting sentiment necessary to the effective working of judicial institutions, and the military forces of the nation took over the task of assuring survival of the nationalism in which Marshall believed. But when the war was over the Court quickly found itself back on the original constitutional highway.

These essays do not specifically appraise the evolution of our constitutional law during the quarter of a century just passed or the unusual behavior of a number of justices in that period in shattering Court unity beyond all precedent and in publicly displaying individual resentments toward the Court. But since with changes in personnel that divisive pattern seems to be disappearing, there is reason for believing that in the long run the public display of mutual respect and the desire to achieve corporate synthesis will be re-established. In any event, the influence of Marshall and his Court has been so tremendous as to merit warmly this token of recognition on the occasion of the two-hundredth anniversary of his birth.

II. Political Questions in the

Virginia of Marshall's Youth

BY DAVID J. MAYS

ONE night in the winter of 1776 George Wythe dropped in to see John Adams to get his views on the kind of governments that should be set up in the American colonies. Both of them were then attending the Congress in Philadelphia. Active hostilities were under way, blood had been shed, Lord Dunmore had been chased out of Norfolk to his nest in the Chesapeake, and a British army was bottled up at Boston. Independence was now being freely discussed, and the character of the government to be set up by the several colonies had become a vital topic. The subject raised by Wythe met an immediate response from Adams, who grew lyrical over the prospect. At Wythe's request, he prepared a letter which was later printed and circulated under the title *Thoughts on Government*. "You and I, my dear friend," he exclaimed, "have been sent into life at a time when the greatest lawgivers of antiquity would have wished to live!" When, he went on, had three million people ever before had "full power and a fair opportunity to form and establish the wisest and happiest government that human wisdom can contrive?"

There were, of course, many other political questions to engage the attention of the people of Virginia during this period—the regulation of tobacco growing and market-ing, which always required long debate in the Committee of the Whole House, and the import taxes on slaves, which the humanitarians and the large planters with surplus Negroes tried to keep high and the new planters on-the-make tried to keep low. But such domestic issues as these had become swallowed up in the contest with Great Britain. The colonists had long insisted upon their constitutional rights as Englishmen, and, when that argu-ment seemed inadequate—as it had become by the time the Congress met in 1774—they had fallen back upon the natural rights of man. In Virginia the Revolutionary forces were led by the large landowners, the aristocratic element, men who desired separation from Britain, but not social revolution, which would have undermined their own privileges and power. Lesser men were as active against Great Britain, but wished social changes as well; and the religious movement, dominated by the Baptists, whose ministers, when denied pulpits, preached in their homes and in the open fields, and when thrown into jail, turned the barred windows into pulpits, was in itself a protest against the established order. No people, of course, could be expected to give all of their thoughts to political ques-tions. Long before the war was over they had been denied many of the most necessary material things of life; they

14

longed once more for their pipes of Madeira and for the feel of British cloth and the smell of British leather.

But in the winter of 1776 the world was young; Patrick Henry's gale had come down from the north bringing the clash of resounding arms; and the people were going forward to their destiny, one that they believed they could determine for themselves. This brings us back to Wythe and John Adams, who were to help carve out the pattern of the future.

In his *Thoughts on Government*, which Adams had written in response to Wythe's request, he reasoned that the people must necessarily act through representatives who "should be in miniature an exact portrait of the people at large." The assembly should be bicameral in order to prevent "fits of humor, avarice and ambition," vices that had appeared in Holland, where the members sought to perpetuate their powers, and in the Long Parliament in England. He believed that there should be a division of powers between the legislature, the executive, and the judiciary and that the executive should have a negative on legislation as well as (with the concurrence of his council) the power to pardon and the right (also with the consent of the council) to name judges and other civil and military officers. The independence of the judges was to be assured by continuing them in office during good behavior.

Adams' recommendations for a strong executive met with considerable favor in Massachusetts, New York, and Pennsylvania, but the people of Virginia, probably because of their experience with Dunmore, had had enough of governors and wished to keep the essential powers of government largely in the hands of the legislature, that is to say, retain governmental powers in the hands of the same men who had, subject to the control of the Royal Governor, long retained them.

Unlike Revolutionary leadership in some other colonies, that in Virginia was retained by the same men who had dominated the House of Burgesses. They represented wealth and social position. They made the cause of the Revolution their own, thereby retaining political control. These men moved from the House of Burgesses into the five pre-Revolutionary conventions in Virginia, and then into the General Assembly. There were casualties along the way, of course, with new people coming in, but the continuity was there. The planters of Tidewater Virginia were determined not to lose their control of government. As I have stated, for them the Revolution was not a democratic movement, but merely a severance of the ties with Britain. Nearly all of them were separationists rather than revolutionists in the social sense; having obtained independence, they wanted to go on in the old ways, and their purpose in the last of the pre-Revolutionary conventions was to fashion a new government which would accomplish this aim.

There were large numbers of people, however, particularly in the Piedmont and transmontane counties of Virginia, who did not desire to see political power concentrated in the hands of the Tidewater aristocracy. But the convention itself was dominated by those long accustomed to govern, and the Constitution which they evolved and proclaimed, without submission to the people, kept the powers where they had been during the colonial period.

Under its terms there was to be a bicameral legislature, the General Assembly: a Senate, whose members were elected by districts, and a House of Delegates, whose members were elected by counties, with the result that the small Tidewater counties, more numerous than those in the west, continued their domination. The House of Delegates was everything, or almost everything, since it alone could originate legislation. The Governor was elected by the joint ballot of the two houses; he had no veto power, no power to prorogue or adjourn the Assembly or to dissolve it, and no power to nominate judges. Such powers as he had could be exercised only with the consent of the Privy Council of eight members who were elected by the House and Senate, and he was required to keep a journal for the legislators' inspection at all times.

It was thought that Patrick Henry would be the first Governor of Virginia, as events proved, and he was much upset over the limitations placed upon the executive power. The governorship would be a "mere phantom," as he put it, as indeed it was.

That same convention debated long and earnestly the provisions of the Bill of Rights, drafted by a committee presided over by Archibald Cary, but the handiwork was largely that of George Mason. Mason had had both gout and election troubles, and he did not arrive until May 17, but his presence was immediately felt, and the Bill of Rights adopted by the convention was essentially in accordance with his draft. The accounts of the drafting and adoption of this document as a part of the Constitution are conflicting and unsatisfactory and were written long afterward. Mr. Irving Brant, in his first volume on Madison, has done the best job of any historian in reconciling them, but the fact remains that our information concerning this document is all too meager. Patrick Henry was very critical, as was Thomas Ludwell Lee, of the "aristocrats" who dominated the convention and who, inferentially, were determined to throttle democracy. Since there were no reports of speeches in any Virginia convention until 1788, we know almost nothing of the positions taken by the various members, but Lee's criticism of the "aristocrats" for debating for several days over the first line of the proposed Bill of Rights seems unjustified. Lee, writing to his brother, Richard Henry Lee, on the first of June, asserted that

a certain set of "aristocrats" . . . have kept us at bay on the first line which declares all men to be born equally free and independent. A number of absurd or non-meaning alterations have been proposed. The words as they stand are approved by a very great majority, yet by a thousand master fetches and stratagems, the business has been so delayed that the first clause stands unassented to by the Convention.

The sentence referred to began with the words, "That all men are by nature equally free and independent and have certain inherent rights, of which they cannot, by any compact, deprive or divest their posterity . . ."

I have found no evidence that the "aristocrats" were opposed to this sentence except on the ground that its language was so sweeping that it would free the slaves. At any rate, they went along with it when the president of the convention inserted the words, "when they enter into a state of society," so that the first article of the Bill of Rights in its final form reads:

That all men are by nature equally free and independent and have certain inherent rights, of which, when they enter into a state of society, they cannot, by any compact, deprive or divest their posterity, namely, the enjoyment of life and liberty, with the means of acquiring and possessing property, and pursuing and obtaining happiness and safety.

The slaves had not entered into "a state of society," so the difficulty presented by Mason's draft was obviated. With this out of the way there seem to have been no lengthy contests over the other provisions of the committee's draft.

The new government in Virginia was largely a parliamentary government. The judicial system, having been created entirely by legislative acts, had to carve its own place of dignity and power under the new system. Because of the evolution of the Virginia courts and their imprint upon the law and young Marshall, it is appropriate that a few minutes be devoted to them.

In the judicial system, while the doctrine of the separation of powers was recognized, no provision was made in the Constitution for courts, and it was three years after the Constitution was adopted before the Supreme Court was set up under an act of the General Assembly. This is worthy of emphasis in the light of subsequent developments, when the Supreme Court of Virginia had before it the question of whether it had the power to declare void unconstitutional acts of the General Assembly.

The question of whether or not a court had the power and the duty to declare a legislative act void where it deemed the act unconstitutional was agitated in Virginia for many years before the question came before the Supreme Court of the United States, there to be decided by John Marshall. Not only was the question raised in pamphlets and correspondence, but the county courts had the question before them at least as early as the Parsons' Cause in 1762, and the whole subject became acute in 1765 upon the passage of the Stamp Act. That is an old story. In order to raise revenue from the colonies, Lord Grenville had required stamps on almost any kind of legal document. The county courts in Virginia were determined not to submit to the use of stamps. In order to avoid it, many of the courts closed down altogether. Others remained open in order to handle cases which did not involve the use of stamps. Some others remained open and transacted any business where the parties were willing to take the risk of acting without the accursed stamps. Mobs might march to threaten violence to the sellers of stamps and to confiscate the stamps themselves, but judges had a responsibility, for they knew well that where they took important actions without stamps they not only ran risks themselves, but they also left in serious doubt the legal effect of their actions, with possible grave results to the litigants.

After the protests had been sent to His Majesty and to Parliament, and it became clear that there was no disposition in England to repeal the act, some of the counties met the constitutional issues squarely. In the county court of Accomac the clerk was instructed to proceed without the use of stamps in any case, on the ground that the act was unconstitutional. A few days later the county court of Caroline took the same action, and as far as we know, it did so without having learned of the action taken in Accomac.

All during the decade preceding the Revolution there were many expressions in America to the effect that Parliament had no authority to tax the colonies since they had no representation in Parliament, although it must be remembered that in the First Continental Congress the members were aware that they might not be able to stand safely on that ground and took refuge in the laws of nature in predicating their resistance to the ministry.

In 1782, in the case of *Caton v. Commonwealth*, the question came before the newly constituted Supreme Court of Virginia; in fact, it was the first case that Court ever heard. Three men in Princess Anne County had been convicted of treason and pardoned by resolution of one house of the General Assembly but not by the other, and in construing the act under which the attempted pardon was granted, there was serious question as to whether or not it was violative of the Virginia Constitution. The matter was deemed of such importance that the president of the Court asked all the members of the bar to express themselves freely, irrespective of whether they represented any parties before the Court. The case was one of great celebrity. The members of the General Assembly then in Richmond waiting for a quorum were spectators in the courtroom. Among the young men in town was John Marshall, who was almost certainly there also.

Three different attitudes on the question of constitutionality were asserted by the judges. Some, as in the case of Judge Edmund Pendleton, expressed the view that the constitutional question was not involved and that the Court should not express itself on that point. Others, Judge George Wythe among them, took the position that the constitutional question was not involved, but whenever it did become involved, the Court should declare void any act that it deemed unconstitutional. It was in this case that Judge Wythe made his eloquent and often-quoted pronouncement on the ultimate authority of the Constitution. One of the judges, Judge James Mercer, went all the way, although his opinion has been long buried in Edmund Pendleton's notes and never got into Call's *Reports*. Mercer found that there was a conflict between the act and the Constitution, and that the Court had the power and the duty under such circumstances to declare the act void, and he proceeded to do so.

In 1788, the General Assembly of Virginia reorganized the Supreme Court and attempted to place upon its judges burdens which had not theretofore been imposed upon them. The judges unanimously took the position that this was an unconstitutional act and prepared the famous Remonstrance, which was duly communicated to the Governor and published widely in the press. Governor John Randolph, realizing the seriousness of the situation, called a meeting of the General Assembly to consider the Remonstrance. The General Assembly, meeting immediately after the adjournment of the Virginia Federal Convention, called for the ratification of the federal Constitution, recognized the justice of the position of the judges, and enacted legislation which omitted the objectionable features about which the judges had complained.

It was between the time of the Remonstrance and the action of the General Assembly taken thereon that the Virginia Federal Convention was held in Richmond. Probably the most controversial part of the proposed federal Constitution was that dealing with the judiciary. On the one hand, many asserted in debate that the people of Virginia would be thrown into federal jails, that they would be dragged hundreds of miles to be tried among people to whom they were unknown, and that the courts

would be flagrant instruments of tyranny in a great consolidated national government. Others urged that the
courts could never become tyrannical since they did not
control the purse or the sword and that their strength and
authority would depend solely upon a continued series of
wise and just adjudications. They urged that the courts in
the federal system would prove the last bulwark of liberty.

Along with the president of the convention, young
Marshall, then thirty-two years of age, had the burden of
sustaining this portion of the Constitution in debate. He
knew of the Parsons' Cause, of the action of the county
courts during the Stamp Act troubles, of *Caton* v. *Commonwealth*, and the Remonstrance of the judges. There
was no doubt at all in his mind that the courts had the
power to declare an unconstitutional act void, and he
boldly declared that principle on the convention floor. It
summarized the position of those who shared his views,
and ultimately it was to find expression in his own opinions
in the Supreme Court of the United States.

Here, because of the limitations of time, and because I
might otherwise trespass upon the subjects allotted to
others, I shall bring these observations to a close. I have
said nothing new, but have sought to remind the reader
of certain events which will serve as a prelude to the
papers of the distinguished historians who will follow me.

III. John Marshall as Politician

and Political Theorist

BY ARTHUR N. HOLCOMBE

JOHN MARSHALL'S bicentennial birthday celebration
supplies a timely occasion for re-examining his position
in the history of American political thought. The occasion
is timely, because Marshall has long been regarded as one
of the great American conservatives—Beveridge indeed
eventually called him an ultraconservative—and now the
nature of American conservatism is being reconsidered,
and the contributions of conservative Americans to our
stock of ideas are being reappraised. For many years there
was a taboo in American politics against the word "conservative." Politically conscious Americans, even the most
conservative ones, preferred to call themselves liberals.
Now at last the meaning of the word "liberal" has been
stretched so far and wide and thin that it is losing its
utility, at least in politics, and there are impressive signs

of a revival of interest in conservatism under its own proper name.

If conservatism be defined as a tendency or disposition to maintain existing institutions or views, whatever they may happen to be, Marshall's standing as a conservative would appear to be questionable. He first made a wide reputation for himself in the Virginia Ratifying Convention of 1788 as a leading advocate of the adoption of the new federal Constitution. But this new Constitution was technically a revolutionary document, and in the struggle for ratification the genuine conservatives—in the strictly political sense of the term—were the opponents of ratification under the leadership of the Anti-Federalists, notably Patrick Henry, George Mason, and Governor George Clinton of New York. Henry indeed insisted that he was the true Federalist and that the self-styled Federalists were what we would now call dangerous subversives, bent on the destruction of the established constitutional governments in the states. Marshall not only fought hard for this constitutional revolution, but also devoted the greater part of his public life to strengthening and consolidating the new system of government, partly federal and partly national, which was already stronger and more consolidated than was really desired by most of his fellow Virginians and also at first probably by most Americans.

If conservatism be defined in broader and more philosophical terms as steadfast love of authority and tradition, regardless of the forms they may take in particular situations, Marshall's claims to the title of "conservative" are again questionable. He was by no means personally opposed to all change or innovation. He shared with other leading Virginians of his time, regardless of party, the repugnance to the institution of Negro slavery which led him to support in his later years various schemes for gradual emancipation and to accept the presidency of the Virginia Colonization Society. Nor did he approve of an established church. Although he attended the services of the Richmond Episcopal Church, perhaps out of deference to his wife, he never became a communicant and seems to have inclined toward Unitarianism, which in his time was a radically liberal, if not actually subversive, creed. Though certainly not what is known technically as a freethinker, he was clearly addicted to freedom of thought. Respect for time-honored institutions did not prevent him from acting upon some of his liberal ideas when he deemed action necessary and proper.

A good test of the character of Marshall's conservatism is his attitude toward the unquestionably liberal ideas of his third cousin, once removed, and greatest political antagonist, Thomas Jefferson. Jefferson immortalized the three leading principles of popular government by writing them into the Declaration of Independence, where they will stand through the ages as the finest expression of liberal thought in the field of politics. These principles relate specifically to the purpose of government, the governmental process, and the governmental performance. The first of the three is, in Jefferson's words, that governments are instituted among men to secure the unalienable rights of the people. The test of Marshall's conservatism, therefore, begins with an examination of his opinion concerning the relative importance, among the objectives of government in a free country, of protecting the people's natural rights.

Marshall's first opportunity to disclose the trend of his

thinking on this basic issue of politics came when he was first elected to the Virginia legislature as a popular young war veteran and impecunious lawyer in search of clients. Jefferson was already developing his great reform program in state politics of which in his own opinion the finest fruit was the Virginia Statute of Religious Freedom. Marshall, however, though like Jefferson a liberal in matters of religion, showed no special interest in the disestablishment of the Anglican church in Virginia. On the contrary, his primary concern seemed to be the protection of the rights of veterans and the promotion of sound business-like methods of carrying on the affairs of the commonwealth. These are of course legitimate and laudable activities for a young war veteran in state politics, and the youthful Marshall was indeed a spectacular success in the Virginia legislature. But there is no evidence to support the view that he regarded the protection of the people's natural rights as the primary purpose of the state government. On the other hand, he seemed to have no objection to the separation of church and state. Did his apparent indifference to the political status of organized religion impair his title to a place among the genuine conservatives? Modern conservative writers such as Professor Russell Kirk would apparently have to answer this question in the affirmative.

Marshall's second outstanding opportunity to show his interest in popular rights came with his election in 1788 to the Virginia Ratifying Convention called to consider the ratification of the new federal Constitution. A leading issue in this convention was the amendment of the Constitution by the adoption of a Bill of Rights designed to afford additional protection for the rights of the people.

Marshall, although he was the principal spokesman for the Federalist members in the debate over the provisions of the Constitution relating to the new judicial system, did not advocate the adoption of a Bill of Rights, except as a concession to the opposition for the sake of winning over votes for ratification. On the contrary, his primary concern was for a national system of courts which could offer greater security to the special interests of businessmen and property owners. This was not exactly the role of a political thinker constitutionally opposed to change and innovation, but neither was it the way an ardent Jeffersonian would have exploited the opportunity afforded by a leading position in such a convention.

The second of Jefferson's principles of popular government, as expressed by him in the Declaration of Independence, is that governments derive their just powers from the consent of the governed. In 1776 this was not only a revolutionary doctrine in the British Empire but also a subversive one in the Old Dominion itself. Judged by this principle, the first constitution of Virginia was seriously defective, as Jefferson himself complained in his *Notes on the State of Virginia*. One of his most cherished projects of political reform was to make the state constitution more democratic. But Marshall from the beginning of his career in Virginia politics manifested a deeper interest in putting constitutional limitations upon the authority of the legislature than in making it more representative of the people.

The development of his thinking on this subject is clearly revealed in his *Autobiographical Sketch*, written for Justice Story in 1827. "When I recollect the wild and enthusiastic democracy with which my political opinions of that day were tinctured," Marshall confessed to his most trusted associate on the Supreme Court, "I am disposed to ascribe my devotion to the union, and to a government competent to its preservation, at least as much to casual circumstances as to judgment." The circumstances to which he referred were above all his military experience in the Revolutionary War:

I partook largely of the sufferings and feelings of the army, and brought with me into civil life an ardent devotion to its interests. My immediate entrance into the state legislature opened to my view the causes which had been chiefly instrumental in augmenting those sufferings, and the general tendency of state politics convinced me that no safe and permanent remedy could be found but in a more efficient and better organized general government. The questions, too, which were perpetually recurring in the state legislatures, and which brought annually into doubt principles which I thought most sound, . . . gave a high value in my estimation to that article in the constitution which imposes restrictions on the states.

Thus, in Marshall's mind, the great attraction of the new federal Constitution was not the establishment of a national House of Representatives, with the accompanying bright prospect of an enhanced responsibility to the people of the United States by a more serviceable general government, but the darker prospect, as it seemed to Anti-Federalists, of restrictive constitutional limitations upon the popular branches of the state governments.

The quality of Marshall's conservative mind was more sharply revealed by the struggle with the Jeffersonians over Washington's Neutrality Proclamation and the Jay Treaty. "We were all strongly attached to France," Marshall declared years later in his memoir for Justice Story, "scarcely any man more strongly than myself. I sincerely believed human liberty to depend in great measure on the success of the French Revolution." But he resented even more strongly French intervention in American affairs and presently came to feel that, as he expressed it, "our independence was brought into real danger by the overgrown and inordinate influence of France." When his ablest leader in the battle for ratification of the Federal Constitution in the Convention of 1788, James Madison, went over to the Jeffersonians, Marshall quickly became the most aggressive and influential Federalist in Virginia politics. President Washington would have appointed him to succeed his early friend and fellow veteran, James Monroe, in the legation at Paris, if Marshall had been willing to interrupt his law practice. In world politics, as in those of his own state, Marshall preferred the maintenance of a balance of power to the vindication of government by consent of the governed.

But Marshall's opposition to the growth of French power did not lead him into the camp of the pro-British party. He liked Fisher Ames, George Cabot, Theodore Sedgwick, and the other Massachusetts Federalists, whom he soon came to know at the seat of government in Philadelphia, but when the great rupture came between them and President John Adams, he took his stand with Adams and supported the mission under Chief Justice Oliver Ellsworth designed to do for Franco-American relations what Chief Justice John Jay had been sent to do for our relations with Great Britain. If addiction to the Anglomania of the late 1790's be the test of conservatism in American politics at the close of the Federalist period, Marshall was no ultraconservative like Alexander Hamilton, though he greatly admired Hamilton, but was definitely a member of the moderate conservative faction headed by Adams. He could even see the political folly of the Alien and Sedition Acts, whatever may have been his opinion concerning their constitutionality. In modern terminology he was at this time a rightist, but his position lay closer to the right of center than to the far right.

The third Jeffersonian principle of popular government, which may be employed to test the quality of the conservatism of John Marshall, was expressed in the right of revolution. Jefferson's indulgent attitude toward Shays' Rebellion showed that he could put a literal interpretation upon this ultimate resort of a sovereign people, but when his own turn came to lead a revolution in the domestic politics of the United States his instrument was not an armed rabble but a shrewdly organized and disciplined political party. Happily the American two-party system has introduced a degree of moderation in the use of political power, and of responsiveness to the changing moods of the people, that has made the right of voting in our presidential and congressional elections a more than fair equivalent for the inconvenient and unreliable right of revolution. Perhaps Jefferson, no more than Washington, foresaw the elaborate development and functional efficiency of the two-party system, but he was quick to perceive the importance of party organization in a popular government, operating on the continental scale of American politics, and to devise a practical method of party government. Marshall, on the other hand, was much slower to understand the revolutionary role of party government.

Marshall's conservatism in dealing with the unplanned

institution of organized partisanship was disclosed in his correspondence with Hamilton at the time of the disputed presidential election of 1800. Forced to choose between Jefferson and Burr, most of the Federalists preferred the latter on grounds of political expediency. Marshall, who knew too little about Burr and perhaps too much about Jefferson, was disposed to go along with the bulk of his party. To Hamilton, who urged him to accept Jefferson as the lesser of the two evils, he replied that Jefferson's "foreign prejudices" seemed to him totally to unfit Jefferson for the presidency. "In addition to this solid and immovable objection," Marshall continued, "Mr. Jefferson appears to me to be a man who will embody himself with the House of Representatives," and, "by weakening the office of President . . . sap the fundamental principles of the government, and become the leader of that party which is about to constitute the majority of the legislature."

Marshall objected to a President who would put himself at the head of his party in the Congress. This now seems a strange aberration, coming from a man who had no objection to the excursions into politics of Chief Justices Jay and Ellsworth, who only mildly discountenanced bitterly partisan political harangues by Federalist judges to captive audiences of jurymen, and who was soon to be busily engaged in making out a big batch of judicial commissions for Federalist politicians who, defeated at the polls, would seek refuge in the national judiciary; and he himself held concurrently the high offices of Secretary of State and Chief Justice. But it was not inconsistent with the principles of a political thinker who would have distrusted organized partisanship all the more if he had understood it to be the most effective means of making a system of constitutional government more democratic than had been intended by its original framers. Perhaps Marshall, who had a practical rather than theoretical cast of mind, did intuitively perceive the natural tendency of party government under the federal Constitution. Be that as it may, he undoubtedly subscribed to Adams' theory of the presidency, and believed that Presidents, like Chief Justices, should stand above factious partisanship but surrender no portion of their claims to high political as well as judicial authority.

Years later, writing to Justice Story on the eve of the campaign in which Andrew Jackson was to wrest the presidency from the son of Marshall's closest political friend, Marshall revealed the somber hue of his latest reflections on government in a democracy:

I begin to doubt whether it will be long practicable peaceably to elect a chief magistrate possessing the powers which the constitution confers on the President of the United States, or such powers as are necessary for the government of this great country with a due regard to its essential interests. I begin to fear that our constitution is not doomed to be so long lived as its real friends have hoped. What may follow sets conjecture at defiance. I shall not live to witness and bewail the consequences of those furious passions which seem to belong to men.

In his early manhood he had expressed similar doubts, when depressed by the news of Shays' Rebellion. "I fear," he wrote, "and there is no opinion more degrading to the dignity of man, that those have truth on their side who say that man is incapable of governing himself."

But, one may ask, did Marshall really believe what he was writing in these moods of depression? He was not discouraged by Shays' Rebellion from fighting for the

33

ratification of the Constitution, nor was he discouraged by the rough violence of Jacksonian democracy from continuing the struggle to give the Constitution the construction which he deemed to be in the public interest. He never, like John Jay, came to despise the high office in which he contended for so many years with his political opponents; nor did he ever, like Alexander Hamilton, lose faith in what Hamilton eventually called a frail and worthless fabric; nor did he, like Gouverneur Morris, finally despair of a republic governed by untutored rustics and wild westerners. Despite his fears, he clung to his office as long as life permitted in the hope that Jackson's successors, like Jefferson's, would be more reasonable and appoint an acceptable Chief Justice in his place. Whatever he may have written, when temporarily depressed, his naturally sanguine temper forbade him to give up hope for a better state of the Union.

We may conclude that Marshall's record of opposition to Jeffersonianism clearly entitles him to high rank among American conservatives, but how should he be rated on a scale that distinguishes between right of center and far right? Beveridge, who apparently gave some thought to questions of this kind, wrote in one place that "no man in America was less democratic in his ideas of government" than Marshall, and he devoted a chapter to Marshall's services in the Virginia Constitutional Convention of 1829 under the title "The Supreme Conservative." Only a statesman of the far right could be described as Beveridge describes his hero at this time.

But our most recent writer on American conservatism, Professor Clinton Rossiter, is more discriminating. John Marshall, according to Professor Rossiter, was no "hide-bound" Tory, like Fisher Ames, or "plutocratic" Tory, like Hamilton. He did not belong to what Rossiter calls that "hard core of Rightists," that is, the "die-hard Federalists." In the Virginia Convention of 1829 Marshall was associated with time-honored Jeffersonians, notably Madison and Monroe, in seeking viable compromises between the far right and the left. Old Federalists and old Jeffersonians together threw themselves into the unequal struggle against universal suffrage and unchecked majority rule. Such men stood manifestly to the right of center, indeed well to the right, but on ground definitely falling short of the far right. Marshall, like Madison and Monroe at this stage of their careers, if we accept Rossiter's terminology, must be pronounced a "genuine Conservative" rather than a "reactionary Rightist."

A final question still remains. Is Rossiter's classification of political types the most convenient for a political scientist? Rossiter's list of the "twenty-one points" of the conservative tradition supplies an attractive picture of what is certainly a useful and even admirable type of citizen in a free country. But does it describe active politicians and accepted statesmen in the most realistic terms? Conservatism, Rossiter writes, "is a wondrous mosaic of opinions about man's essence and experience," and he adds, "The mortar that holds together the mosaic of Conservatism is religious feeling." He quotes with approval Professor Russell Kirk's dictum that the first canon of conservative thought is the belief that "a divine intent rules society as well as conscience." But Marshall showed no interest in theological interpretations of history. Indeed, he was rather casual about religion. The rights of property rather than the interests of religion formed the chief component in his brand of conservatism. Perhaps, as Madison persuasively argued in the celebrated tenth number of *The Federalist*, differences over property rather than religious attitudes should be recognized as forming the usual basis of partisanship, and hence also of the political classification of politicians and statesmen.

But these reflections threaten to carry me further than I should attempt to go on this occasion. I must be content with a final reflection on the place of John Marshall in the history of American political thought. The conflict between his views and those of his great political opponent, Jefferson, seems to me to have been exaggerated by partisan historians. The two men, to be sure, were for a time prime antagonists in the struggle between two great parties. There was some justification for Jefferson's suspicion that Marshall's *Life of Washington* was designed to be a secret weapon in the partisan struggle, though to the present generation a natural desire to make some needed and easy money seems to be a more significant explanation of Marshall's unfortunate venture into the literary world. Marshall, like his predecessor in the chief justiceship, Ellsworth, was a leading member of the moderate or Adams faction of Federalists at the turn of the century and the leading Federalist in office after the triumph of the Jeffersonians. Unlike his temperamental chieftain, Marshall never became reconciled with the great apostle of the "wild and enthusiastic democracy" of his youth. Jefferson and Adams could distinguish between the natural and the artificial aristocracy and could comfort themselves after their final retirement from active politics with the thought that it was to the former and not to the latter kind of aristocracy that they both really belonged. But Marshall was not interested in these theoretical distinctions and seemed content with such a place in the aristocracy, natural or artificial, as was fitting for a valiant officer in the Revolutionary War and a leading member of the great Fairfax land syndicate. He must of course be placed to the right on a modern scale of political attitudes, as Jefferson must be placed to the left. Both of these great Virginians and Americans, however, abhorred extremes, and could not hold for long to a political course deviating widely from the natural center, where tradition and reason meet and make the necessary adjustments to the circumstances of the time and the temper of the people.

IV. John Marshall and the

Lawyers and Politicians

BY IRVING BRANT

NO GREAT talent is required, a century and a quarter after John Marshall's death, to recognize the elements of greatness in his personality and in his achievements. He was forty-six—rather old by the standards of his day—when President John Adams sent his name to the Senate, but his pre-eminent fitness for the judiciary had been proclaimed long before that. Marshall was only thirty-seven when he was first recommended for the bench. The suggestion came from a shrewd judge of men and measures, though hardly from a source that would be anticipated. It came from Thomas Jefferson.

That was away back in 1792, when Jefferson was Secretary of State and Marshall was known to but few men outside of his native state. Hearing that Alexander Hamilton had expressed a strong desire to see John Marshall enter Congress, Jefferson wrote to James Madison, "I am told that Marshall has expressed half a mind to come. Hence I conclude that Hamilton has plied him well with flattery and solicitation and I think nothing better could be done than to make him a judge." [1]

If that excellent suggestion had been carried to fulfillment, it would have meant the election of Marshall one year later to succeed James Mercer on the Virginia Court of Appeals. With equal fatality, the quick demonstration of his talents on that court should have led his friend and admirer, President Washington, to nominate him for Chief Justice when John Jay resigned in 1795. In that event, benching Marshall to keep him out of the House of Representatives would have lifted him six years earlier to that position of judicial supremacy which must have caused Jefferson to say to himself many times in later years: "Oh, if we could only bury that man in Congress!"

Of course, the word "if" cannot be used to rewrite history. Since Marshall refused to become an associate justice of the United States Supreme Court in 1798, he certainly would have declined a state judgeship in '93. However, the imperative reason for such a refusal will furnish a starting point for consideration of John Marshall and politicians, if not of Marshall and lawyers.

For seven years, beginning in 1793, Marshall's life was charted by an outside force which he was powerless to control. He was ruled by the maturity dates on the promissory notes given by him and three partners for the purchase of the confiscated lands of Lord Fairfax in northern Vir-

[1] Jefferson to Madison, June 29, 1792, *Writings of Thomas Jefferson* (Federal ed.; Washington, D.C., 1905), VII, 130.

ginia.[2] Had there been no Fairfax purchase, Marshall would not have been forced, during the next half-dozen years, to decline both political and judicial offices of high honor and low pay. The avenue would have been open to swift and high advancement in the political field, with who knows what effect upon his own career and the country's history.

Marshall's early alignment with Hamilton did not put him wholly outside the Republican pale. In 1793, when there was friction with Spain over the Mississippi River, Secretary of State Jefferson asked Madison to recommend someone who could be sent to New Orleans as a secret observer of Spanish activities. "Young Marshall," Madison replied, "seems to possess some of the qualifications, but there would be objections of several sorts to him."

Since he suggested Marshall and nobody else, the reference to "several objections" was probably an example of the finesse Madison habitually employed to overcome Jefferson's prejudices. It was equivalent to saying, "I know you don't like Marshall's politics, but—." However, he did

---

[2] The lands of Lord Fairfax originally comprised more than five million acres between the Potomac and Rappahannock Rivers, granted to Lord Culpeper by James II in 1688. In 1782 the Virginia General Assembly sequestered the quitrents and in 1785 abolished them and other seignorial rights. The Fairfax heirs continued to sell lands which had been held by them in fee, contending that these were not comprehended in the 1782 legislation and that the intervention of the 1783 Treaty of Peace protected them from confiscation in 1785. In 1793, John and James Marshall, their brother-in-law Raleigh Colston, and General Henry (Light-Horse Harry) Lee, united to purchase the residue of lands held in fee, about 160,000 acres. The purchase contract was signed in 1794. See "The Fairfax Proprietary," in *Dictionary of American History*, ed. by James Truslow Adams, I, 240, and Albert Beveridge, *The Life of John Marshall* (Boston, 1919), II, 202–211; IV, 147–157.

specify one important obstacle. The secret agent ought to assume the pose of a merchant engaged in foreign trade. That was no role for Lawyer John Marshall.

Three months later Madison's attitude toward Marshall was sharply critical. He could not feel complete confidence in the republicanism of Wilson Cary Nicholas because the latter was embarked on a variety of projects which called for money and lined him with Richmond merchants, and because of his connection and intimacy with Marshall, of whose *disinterestedness* Nicholas professed a very high opinion. Madison went on:

It is said that Marshall, who is at the head of the great purchase from Fairfax, has lately obtained pecuniary aids from the bank [he meant the newly created Bank of the United States] or people connected with it. I think it certain that he must have felt, in the moment of purchase, an absolute confidence in the moneyed interests that will explain him to everyone that reflects, in the active character he is assuming.[3]

At first glance, that comment appears to cover one of the "several objections" felt earlier by Madison, and it was so construed by Marshall's biographer, Beveridge, but there are a number of reasons for doubting that Madison had heard of the Fairfax purchase when he discussed Marshall for the New Orleans mission.[4] But let that pass. If it

[3] Madison to Jefferson, June 17, Sept. 2, 1793, *Writings of James Madison*, ed. by Gaillard Hunt (New York, 1900–1910), VI, 134, 196; Beveridge, II, 100.

[4] Madison's September 2 comment about Nicholas and Marshall was the last of four reports made in response to a June 2 request from Jefferson that he ask Nicholas to use his influence with Attorney General Edmund Randolph (brother-in-law of Nicholas) at a time when Jefferson and Hamilton were contending for Randolph's support in President Washington's Cabinet. On July 22, after Nicho-

was one of the objections, Beveridge missed the whole point of the criticism. Ignoring the main obstacle to the secret mission—the need to pose as a merchant—the biographer wrote:

Three months later Madison revealed one of these "several objections" to Marshall, but the principal one was his sturdy, fighting Nationalism. This "objection" was so intense that anybody who was even a close friend of Marshall was suspected and proscribed by the Republicans. The Jacobin Clubs of Paris were scarcely more intolerant than their disciples in America.

That was truly absurd interpretation. Jefferson and Marshall were made personal enemies by their political differences. Madison and Marshall, we are told by Joseph Story, remained lifelong friends and mutual admirers in spite of the differences that arose between them.[5] Marshall himself left a record of the intense "surprise and mortification" he felt when he heard a report, which happened to be erroneous, that Madison agreed with Jefferson's condemnation of the Court's ruling in *Cohens* v. *Virginia*.[6]

----

las visited Montpelier, Madison wrote: "I discovered no symptoms of heresy." Obviously, the Marshall-Fairfax heresy which he reported on September 2 had not yet entered the appraisal. Furthermore, had Madison known of the Fairfax purchase on June 17, there would have been no reason to mention Marshall for the New Orleans mission at all. A young lawyer who had just staked his financial future on a gigantic land speculation, with the success of it hinging on a legal battle, would be in no situation to bury himself in a distant Spanish colony. Madison to Jefferson, June 13, 17, July 22, Sept. 2, 1793, *Writings of Madison*, VI, 132, 133–134, 136, 196.

[5] Joseph Story, *An Address on Chief Justice Marshall* (1835) (Rochester, N.Y., 1900), pp. 20–21.

[6] Marshall to Story, July 13, 1821, Massachusetts Historical Society, *Proceedings*, 2d ser., XIV, 328. Beveridge, accepting a guess made by the MHS editors, identified the letter referred to by Marshall

In 1793, however, when negotiations touching on Spain, the Southwest, and the Mississippi were concerned, Jefferson, Madison, and Marshall were all sturdy, fighting nationalists. Marshall's nationalism was the one outstanding qualification which, added to his jovial friendliness, his backwoods appearance, physical hardihood, and horseshoe pitching, would have caused Madison to think of him for this highly nationalistic assignment.

Three months later, Marshall and Nicholas were both criticized on the same narrow point—fear that they were in hock to the Hamiltonian money power. According to erroneous report, Marshall was obtaining easy and certain credit in a banking institution whose loans were associated in Republican minds with financial favoritism for political ends.

There was, however, a moneyed interest in which Marshall felt absolute confidence, and the shattering of that confidence produced a crisis in his life. James Marshall, John's brother and partner in the Fairfax venture, married

---

as that of Jefferson to William C. Jarvis, Sept. 28, 1820, which "had just been made public." Actually, publicity was given to an "Extract of a letter from Thomas Jefferson to ——," a fictitious letter "cooked up" (to use Jefferson's own description) out of letters to Archibald Thweatt and John Taylor of Caroline (Jefferson to Judge Roane, June 27, 1821, *Writings of Jefferson*, XII, 202n–203n). In it Jefferson said: "It is a fatal heresy to suppose that either our state governments are superior to the federal, or the federal to the states. . . . In differences of opinion between these different sets of servants, the appeal is to neither, but to their employers peaceably assembled by their representatives in convention." On June 29 Madison gave Roane a contrary opinion: "I have always thought . . . that on the abstract question whether the federal or the state decisions ought to prevail, the sounder policy would yield to the claims of the former." *Writings of Madison*, IX, 66.

the daughter of Robert Morris, the Philadelphia private banker. The financial downfall of Morris, just when the two brothers were counting on his once-limitless credit, reduced John Marshall to absolute dependence on his legal fees—a dependence as ironclad and exacting as any mortgage held by a bank.

The effect on Marshall's political fortunes may be read in what President Washington wrote to Hamilton, his former Secretary of the Treasury, in 1795: "What am I to do for the Secretary of State? . . . Mr. Marshall, of Virginia, has declined the office of Attorney General, and I am pretty certain, would adopt no other."

Two years later the Fairfax notes impelled Marshall to accept President Adams' offer of a special mission to Europe. He guessed correctly that the financial reward would exceed his four-or-five-thousand-dollar income as leader of the Virginia bar. It did. His exposure of the bribe-soliciting XYZ papers electrified the country. He came home a national hero. A Federalist and generous Congress allowed him $19,963.75—"the greatest God-send," Jefferson wrote, "that ever could have befallen a man." This sum, as Beveridge points out, exceeded Marshall's actual expenses by $15,000 and gave him a year's income almost equal to the combined salaries of the President and his entire Cabinet.[7]

The burden of the Fairfax notes fell away. Marshall yielded to the plea of General Washington that he help to save the country from ruin by running for Congress. In the ensuing campaign, Republicans castigated Marshall for speaking too softly against the Alien and Sedition Acts, while rabid New England excoriated him as a semi-Jacobin

[7] Beveridge, II, 209–211, 347, 371–373.

for not committing political suicide by defending those laws. "His character is done for," exclaimed Fisher Ames. He was elected by 108 votes after the old radical Patrick Henry gave him a passionate endorsement, very effective among voters who did not know that age and wealth had converted Henry into an extreme conservative.

Before Congress had been two months in session, Speaker Theodore Sedgwick was praising this new member to the skies. "In short," he wrote, "we can do nothing without him"—quite a tribute from a man who had called Marshall's Alien and Sedition criticism a mean and paltry electioneering trick which aided French villainy. There was little time for Sedgwick to lean on Marshall's shoulder. In five months he was Secretary of State and in another eight months he became Chief Justice.[8]

Thus, by the irony of fate, John Marshall arrived at the exact spot which he might have reached through a different line of march had there been no financial deterrents to a political career. Yet it did not come to the same thing! The difference lies in the political career that was foregone, and the resulting options that were not presented. Had there been no Fairfax notes to meet, Marshall would have gone like a rocket to the highest post in Washington's cabinet. President Adams would have inherited a Secretary of State of unshakable loyalty and sound judgement, instead of that crafty master of intrigue, Timothy Pickering. There would have been no Cabinet cabal against the President, probably no Alien and Sedition Acts.

By the time Marshall finally became Secretary of State, in 1800, the Cabinet feud and policy blunders had reduced the Federalist party to a heap of wreckage. Neither Mar-

[8] *Ibid.*, II, 390, 391, 412, 432.

shall nor any other man could have stemmed the rising tide of Jeffersonian democracy. Nevertheless, had his stabilizing influence been at the core of things throughout the Adams administration, the Federalist party would have entered the 1800 presidential campaign with vastly greater strength and unity. The election of Jefferson would have left Marshall as the idolized leader of a beaten but unshattered party.

Looking into the backward horoscope of alternatives, one can see a mighty battle for the presidency, in 1808, between Marshall and Madison—two Virginians far apart in politics, both of them mental giants, endowed with similar gifts of political finesse, with all the political currents favoring Madison and all the odds of crackerbox appeal on Marshall's side. It would still be possible, today, to put up a few five-dollar bets on the outcome, and Louis Bean could decide the wagers with scientific precision.

Once it is understood why Marshall remained so long on the political side lines, before his appointment to the Supreme Court, it becomes easier to understand why he found it so hard to remain on the side lines, after he became Chief Justice. There can be no doubt about the intensity of his partisanship at the moment of the great transition.

In January 1801, just before his nomination to the Court, Marshall rejected the plea of Alexander Hamilton that he exert his influence for Jefferson, in the breaking of the electoral-college tie by the House of Representatives. The Washington *Federalist*, known to Republicans as Marshall's organ, continued to support Burr ardently. Marshall himself replied to Hamilton that he would stay out of the contest. Burr might be, as Hamilton asserted, more danger-

ous than Jefferson, but Jefferson's "foreign prejudices"—
his friendship for France and enmity to England—totally
unfitted him to be President. In addition, wrote Marshall,
Jefferson would "embody himself with the House of Representatives."

> By weakening the office of President, he will increase his per-
> sonal power. He will diminish his responsibility, sap the founda-
> tion principles of the government, and become the leader of that
> party which is about to constitute the majority of the legislature.
> The morals of the author of the letter to Mazzei cannot be pure.[9]

That last sentence reveals the intensity of feeling that
underlay the argument. Jefferson never made any man more
lastingly bitter against him than he did John Marshall,
when he classified the Federalist leaders as one-time revolutionaries who had turned into Anglicans, monarchists, and
aristocrats—"men who were Samsons in the field and
Solomons in the council, but who have had their heads
shorn by the harlot England." [10]

If Marshall was right about Jefferson, and Hamilton

[9] Marshall to Alexander Hamilton, Jan. 1, 1801, Hamilton, *Works*,
ed. by J. C. Hamilton (New York, 1851), VI, 501–503.

[10] Jefferson to Philip Mazzei, April 24, 1796, *Writings of Jefferson*,
VIII, 240. Beveridge, II, 537, revealed his intense bias by presenting
the quotation about the Samsons and the Solomons with the prefa-
tory words, "Jefferson thus refers to Washington." He thereby, without explanation, converted Federalist accusation into a fact. Also,
remarking that translations of the letter first into Italian, then into
French and again into English produced little change from Jefferson's
original, Beveridge picked the incorrect retranslation, "the whore
England," out of a footnote to the published Jefferson letter and
used it as if that were what Jefferson wrote. For indications (though
not proof) that Jefferson did not have Washington in mind see Irving Brant, *James Madison, Father of the Constitution* (Indianapolis, 1941), 453–454.

47

was right about Burr, the country must be preserved from both of these villains. Marshall's strategy was simple. Let the House of Representatives prolong the deadlock until March 4. The offices of President and Vice President would then be vacant, and since it would have become impossible to fill these offices in the manner prescribed by the Constitution, Congress should determine by law how it was to be done.

The Washington *Federalist* denied that Marshall wrote the article signed "Horatius" in which this plan was broached, but nobody else seemed to have any doubt about it. Beveridge, who would have thundered denunciations if such a plan had been dreamed up by Jefferson against Marshall, was impelled to say of it: "The argument is able and convincing, and it is so perfectly in Marshall's method of reasoning and peculiar style of expression that his authorship of it would appear to be reasonably certain."

This issue became more acute in Marshall's home town when a letter was read aloud in the Richmond coffeehouse citing him as expressing the same opinion to the Secretary of War. This brought Monroe's son-in-law, George Hay, "Hortensius," into action. In the Richmond *Examiner*, the young lawyer challenged Marshall either to defend the proposal in public or disclaim it and thus "rescue your reputation from the odium which it has already incurred." [11]

Marshall kept silent, but over the country the proposal produced such a shaking of pitchforks, scythes, squirrel guns, and goose quills that it may well have helped insure the election of Jefferson. Let us suppose that the scheme

[11] Beveridge, II, 540–544.

had been put into effect and that it gave the country a better President. How would it have affected the presidency itself?

To elect Jefferson President, Marshall had written to Hamilton, would weaken the office, diminish its responsibilities and sap the fundamental principles of the government. Seemingly he did not ask himself whether the presidency would be strengthened or weakened, whether presidential responsibilities would be enlarged or diminished, whether the fundamental principles of the government would be sapped or maintained, by subjecting the constitutional processes of election to congressional intrigue and statutory deviation.

In this fashion, just two weeks before President Adams nominated him for Chief Justice, John Marshall allowed his distrust and dislike of Jefferson to overshadow his respect for the Constitution. Perhaps that explains why, in writing the Court's opinion in *Marbury v. Madison*, the Chief Justice went far out of his way to lay lusty strokes upon the President on an issue rendered moot by the decision itself.

Marshall was surely aware, as the whole country was, that he acted as a political partisan in writing that portion of the Marbury opinion. Perhaps his knowledge of the country's knowledge will explain the mystery of his conduct when he appeared before the Senate as a witness in the impeachment trial of Justice Samuel Chase. The articles of impeachment voted against Chase amounted to a finding by the House of Representatives that partisan misconduct on the bench was a high crime or misdemeanor—constitutional grounds of removal. If ever a man deserved to be booted off the Supreme Court on general principles,

Chase did. But if his misconduct was found to be criminal, any judge could be impeached and removed for political reasons. It was known, moreover, that President Jefferson was pushing the prosecution through his agent in the House, John Randolph. Anybody could sense the logical sequence: Out goes Chase; out goes Marshall.

At such a juncture, with the Chief Justice called as a witness, the Court needed the protection of his manner more than Chase did of his testimony. After he finished, Randolph eulogized him but Federalist Senator William Plumer wrote in his diary: "The Chief Justice really discovered too much caution—too much fear—too much cunning— He ought to have been more bold, frank and explicit than he was. . . . A cunning man ought never to discover the arts of the *trimmer* in his testimony." [12]

As far as Marshall was concerned, the Senate's failure to convict Chase swept away all future personal hazards. Then came the treason trial of Aaron Burr, which caught the Chief Justice's spirit on a high rebound. In the trial of Burr, Chief Justice Marshall and District Judge Cyrus Griffin presided jointly in circuit court at Richmond. President Jefferson, with manifest impropriety, had publicly called Burr guilty of treason before he was arrested and was pushing the prosecution with corresponding zeal. Perhaps, under these circumstances, Marshall was merely defending the courts from executive invasion when, from the bench, he referred to "the hand of malignity" behind the prosecution. Gone was his fear of Jefferson and gone too, apparently, his older fear that Jefferson would weaken the presidency. At any rate, there was no trace of either in the

[12] William Plumer, Diary, Feb. 16, 1805, Plumer Papers, Library of Congress; quoted in Beveridge, III, 196.

subpoena Marshall issued, commanding the President of the United States to appear in court at Richmond and bring certain papers with him. Nor was this action rendered more respectful by the interlocutory opinion in which he studiously insulted the President and belittled the presidency. Image, if you can, Chief Justice Marshall addressing such a paper to President George Washington. He would have been seared to a cinder by his own vision of the fire in Washington's eye. Jefferson sent the papers, ignored the subpoena, and privately denounced the judge.[13]

It is known now that Burr repeatedly sought British aid in splitting the Union by force of arms. Probably he would have been convicted of treason if the dispatches of the British minister could have been laid before the jury.[14] But it would have been a conviction unsupported by constitutional evidence of an overt act, and it would have nullified, in effect, the great service Marshall performed in that trial by striking down the doctrine of constructive treason. The impression made on lawyers as well as the public, that the Chief Justice deliberately protected Burr from the proper fate, was in large part a reflection of Marshall's use of the trial as political propaganda against Jefferson.

The impression of bias sank deep and lasted. "Chief Justice Marshall has it seems acquitted Burr," wrote At-

---

[13] Beveridge, III, 376; Marshall, opinion on the motion for a writ of subpoena duces tecum, to be directed to the President of the United States, *Annals of Congress*, XVII, 693–703; Jefferson to George Hay, June 17, 19, 1807, and undated draft, *Writings of Jefferson*, 400n–407n.

[14] Anthony Merry to Lord Hawkesbury, March 13, 1804, to Lord Harrowby, March 29, 1805, to Lord Mulgrave, April 29, Aug. 4, Nov. 25, 1805, Public Records Office (London), Foreign Office, 5, vol. XLV (transcripts in Library of Congress).

torney General Caesar Rodney when the trial ended.[15] Three years later, when Burr was in Paris, stories began to appear in the British and American press, about the scheme he broached to Police Chief Fouché, that England and France should make peace with each other and divide the United States between them.[16] Hearing that Burr was coming home, the Baltimore *Whig* remarked: "Burr once said, he would turn Jefferson out of the White House, and drive Congress into the Potomac. Perhaps he is returning to fulfil his promise. But we hope he will spare *his friend* Chief Justice Marshall."

Napoleon fired Fouché and refused Burr a passport, and so there was no need to spare the Chief Justice. The most important fact about the item in the *Whig* is the date of it, November 22, 1810. That carries the published appearance of the name "White House" back four years from the 1814 date discovered by Wilhelmus Bryan, author of the *History of Washington*.[17]

The belief that Marshall befriended Burr in the treason trial gained wider currency because of a social event that took place during a momentary lull in the prosecution. To celebrate Marshall's refusal to hold Burr to the grand jury for anything more than a misdemeanor (the jury itself lifted the charge to treason), Defense Counsel John Wick-

[15] Caesar Rodney to Madison, Sept. 16, 1807, Madison Papers, Library of Congress.

[16] Cf. Irving Brant, *James Madison, Secretary of State* (Indianapolis, 1941), 358–359.

[17] Wilhelmus B. Bryan, "The Name White House," Columbia Historical Society (Washington), Records, XXXIII–XXXIV, 306–307. The earliest use of the name "White House" found by Bryan, was in a letter from Francis J. Jackson to Timothy Pickering, April 24, 1811.

ham gave a victory dinner in Burr's honor. Among the guests was the Chief Justice. Beveridge did his best to disparage the statement in James Thayer's *Life of Marshall* that the Chief Justice knew Burr was to be present and regretted afterward that he hadn't taken his wife's advice and stayed away. That tale, said Beveridge, was "probably a myth," ascribed to an unnamed descendant of Marshall and recorded "more than a century" after the incident took place.

True, Professor Thayer's biography was published ninety-four years after the Burr trial, and in round numbers, ninety-four may perhaps be called more than a hundred. But Thayer, born during Marshall's lifetime, was intimately acquainted with his children and grandchildren. Testimony from so responsible a witness would hardly be dismissed as "probably a myth" if he had said the opposite.[18]

Marshall's presence at that dinner was of course improper, but it grew out of his social relationship with lawyers—a bond so close, and so unrelated to the pros and cons of court trials, that the presence of a defendant assumed importance only after the soup was served. For a dozen years before Marshall went onto the Court, he and John Wickham were either opponents or partners in a great proportion of the hard-fought lawsuits in Richmond. Wickham's periodic dinners for lawyers were matched in popularity only by Marshall's dinners for lawyers. The Chief Justice was a man of wit and laughter. Hilarity drowned out politics. The presence of George Hay, the "Hortensius" of newspaper attacks on Marshall, was enough to prove that the tie of the law was stronger than the bar

[18] Beveridge, III, 394–397; James B. Thayer, *Life of John Marshall* (Boston, 1901), 80–81.

of partisanship. Only Spencer Roane was habitually absent from Marshall's table, and he stayed away of his own accord.

Marshall's connections with lawyers and politicians were deeply affected by the Judiciary Act of 1789. We think of Supreme Court justices today as men who live and work in Washington, their old ties of residence totally broken. It was different when the members of the Court rode circuit. Chief Justice Marshall continued to live in Richmond. He sat as a circuit judge in that city and in Raleigh, and he went to Washington each February for a short session of the full Court. As late as 1834, only one member of the Supreme Court was accompanied to Washington by his wife. The other members all roomed and boarded in the same house and gave dinners that were the talk of the national capital.

Living in Richmond, the Chief Justice continued to entertain lawyers and state judges in festive style. Noted visitors came from other states—the great rivals Luther Martin and William Pinkney, who forgot their clients at Marshall's table. Their heralded appearance made the courtroom a gathering place of society.[19]

In the age groups at these dinners one can follow the successive generations of Virginia lawyers. There were those to whom Marshall himself was a youngster—Chancellor Wythe, under whom he studied; Judge Pendleton, Judge Blair, Patrick Henry, Paul Carrington, and those sour and sweet Scotchmen, Alexander McRae and "Old Jock" Warden. Then came the lawyers of Marshall's own generation—Edmund Randolph, John Wickham, Bushrod Wash-

[19] Beveridge, IV, 77–78; Mary V. H. Terhune, *Some Colonial Homesteads and Their Stories* (New York, 1912), 85–87.

ington, John Taylor of Caroline. And after them came the
new young men to whom Marshall was a veteran—such
men as William Wirt, Benjamin Botts, and George Hay,
all of whom were junior counsel, and not all on the same
side, in the trial of Burr.

The state courts, in that day, were more venerable than
the federal. As a lawyer, Marshall argued before elderly
state judges. On the supreme bench, in the first decade of
his service, young lawyers appeared before young justices.
The average age of the members of the Supreme Court
in 1811 was only forty-three years. But the time came when
this situation had changed, and William Wirt was old
enough and wise enough to give this advice to his own
lawyer son-in-law: Avoid flowery oratory; imitate Marshall's
simple process of reasoning.[20]

John Marshall's continued residence in Richmond, and
his social life there, made it easier for him to remain active
in politics. We find him in 1808 dreading the threatened
calamity of Madison's election as President. The changes
made and threatened by a despotic party, he wrote in
September to the Federalist candidate for President, must
give serious alarm to every intelligent observer. But even
worse was the threat from overseas. If the United States,
obeying the order of Bonaparte, were to enter the French
system of commercial warfare against England, the country no longer would be independent and would infallibly
bring about its own ruin.

Since the whole Federalist party looked on Madison as
the tool of Bonaparte, Marshall can hardly be blamed for
sharing the delusion. He adopted it with reluctance. In

[20] Cf. David J. Mays, *Edmund Pendleton* (Cambridge, Mass.,
1952), II, 281–286, 297–301; Beveridge, II, 193.

that campaign, Madison ran against three opponents, two of them from his own party, and one of these, James Monroe, from his own state. Realizing that the Federalist candidate, Charles Cotesworth Pinckney, had no chance, Marshall helped throw the Virginia Federalists to Monroe. Forming "a small and oppressed minority," the Chief Justice wrote apologetically to the deserted Pinckney, they had no other way to exert influence. Probably, he said, they would have chosen to support Madison because of his superior ability, except for evidence that he was even more prejudiced in foreign affairs than Monroe or Clinton.[21]

One year of Madison as President confirmed all of Marshall's fears. Summarizing, in a letter to Josiah Quincy, the intransigent hostility of France to American shipping, he said he had supposed that this "would have exhausted to the dregs our cup of servility and degradation; but these measures appear to make no impression on those to whom the United States confide their destiny."

The President, to whom these remarks applied, was just then proving his servility to Napoleon by writing, "The late confiscations by Bonaparte comprise robbery, theft, and breach of trust, and exceed in turpitude any of his enormities not wasting human blood." [22] The difference was that Madison saw greater damage coming from another source, while Marshall, overwhelmed by hatred and fear of France, closed his eyes to British aggressions which swept the Federalist party out of power, that spring of 1810, in all but one of the New England states.

[21] Marshall to Charles Cotesworth Pinckney, Sept. 21, Oct. 19, 1908, Pinckney Papers, Library of Congress.

[22] Marshall to Josiah Quincy, April 23, 1810, in Edmund Quincy, *Life of Josiah Quincy* (Boston, 1867), 204; Madison to Jefferson, May 25, 1810, *Writings of Madison*, VIII, 102.

In 1812, after the United States declared war on England, Ben Stoddert of the Adams Cabinet proposed Marshall for President—the only man, he asserted, who had a chance to defeat President Madison. It may be doubted that Marshall would have given up his judicial post without far better prospects than those presented to him, but at least his heart was in the wrong place. Five weeks after the war began, ten days after Stoddert's appeal was published, the Chief Justice wrote to Madison's discharged Secretary of State, Robert Smith, violently assailing the administration and calling on all good men to forget party lines and oppose the continuation of the war. Of course, there may have been no presidential ambition in this, even though all the world knew that Robert Smith was working to depose Madison from the leadership of their party.[23]

One thing can be said for Marshall's position in 1812. If he was not aloof from politics, he was at least aloof from good politics. The Federalist party adopted his platform as the way to victory and found it the road to oblivion.

The destruction of the political party for which he felt affection and loyalty made it easier thereafter for the Chief Justice to steer a nonpartisan course. It blotted out that ambivalence which tied him at once to parochial New England federalism and to the nationalism of the American West. There was, however, a less personal reason for this change in his conduct. The war which he hated and whose results he feared did just the opposite of what he expected from it. Instead of tying the United States to the tail of France, it gave the American people a new feeling of inde-

[23] Beveridge, IV, 31–36.

pendence and a new sense of destiny. They held up their heads in the face of the world and set out to conquer and populate a continent.

Thus, in the minds and spirit of the people, there developed the popular counterpart of that high nationalism which Marshall himself personified in the Supreme Court. The Court became in effect a government in microcosm, with himself at the head of it, immune to the local pulls and hauls of representative democracy, but in full harmony with its ultimate goals.

In the six years from 1819 through 1824 came that swift succession of decisions by the Court and opinions by Marshall which established forever the national character of the United States—*McCulloch* v. *Maryland, Cohens* v. *Virginia, Gibbons* v. *Ogden, Osborn* v. *Bank of the United States.* Those decisions spurred lawyers and politicians to bitter protest, especially in Virginia. Judging the country by the polemics of press and legislatures, one might suppose that the Supreme Court was defying the main current of public opinion. In truth it was protected by the very nationalism which it was fostering. This was all part of a national development which was seen with remarkable clarity by a young French diplomat at the close of the War of 1812. Each of the two great parties, reported Chargé d'Affaires Roth in 1816, was ready to adopt the doctrines of the other in order to promote its own popularity and power.

In the midst of this clash or rather this fusion of political principles, abandoned or resumed, the government of this country, Federalist or Republican, moves with great steps toward an extension of strength and power which insensibly changes its nature. . . . By the advance of civilization, the increase in the revenues of the states and the development of wealth and industry, those free and rude habits which belong to the early age of society will be relegated to a lower class, neither the Federalist nor the Republican party, but which will be subject to the rule of the one or the other. . . . There will result from this concentration a greater strength of union, and there will be less to fear from the tearings and slashings which democratic license would necessarily produce and unduly prolong.[24]

This opinion, said young M. Roth, was not openly avowed, but he had glimpsed it in the most important men of both parties.

Here, then, was not only the driving force behind Marshall's greatest opinions, but the protective cover against the counterassaults of Jefferson, Judge Roane, John Taylor, Editor Ritchie and others who inveighed against the Supreme Court's nationalism. Here was the force that made Andrew Jackson a nationalist in spite of his states' rightism, when South Carolina, protesting the tariff but thinking of slavery, carried its constitutional challenge to the point of nullification and the threat of secession. Here was the impulse that caused member after member of the Supreme Court, appointed by Jefferson and Madison from the ranks of the Republican party, to join with Marshall in exalting national authority.

And this brings us to a relationship between Marshall and the lawyers which infinitely transcends the social ties among them. When William Pinkney, Daniel Webster, and William Wirt appeared for the United States and the Second Bank in *McCulloch* v. *Maryland*,[25] they were op-

[24] Roth to the Duc de Richelieu, April 5, 1816, Archives des Affaires Etrangères (Paris), Correspondance politique, Etats-Unis, LXXIII, 6–10 verso (photostats in Library of Congress).

[25] 4 Wheat. 316 (1819).

posed by men of almost equal renown in the law though
not in politics—Luther Martin, Joseph Hopkinson, and
Walter Jones. But Pinkney, Webster, and Wirt were the
spokesmen of the America that emerged from the War of
1812. When Chief Justice Marshall drew so heavily upon
Pinkney and Webster for his opinion in that case, and
when he merged his reasoning with Webster's in defining
the breadth of the commerce power, he was not merely
reducing his own labor through the talents of gifted lawyers. He was completing a partnership in American destiny.

Great lawyers and great statesmen do not jump full
grown from the forehead of Zeus. The John Marshall who
manipulated opinions and orders to throw obloquy on
President Jefferson was not the same man whose broad
vision, courage, and clear thinking cause the American
people to honor him two hundred years after his birth.
Growth is the living principle of greatness. The greatness
of John Marshall lies in the fact that he grew with the
nation, while he helped it grow.

V. Judicial Review and

the Maintenance of the

Federal System

BY F. D. G. RIBBLE

JOHN MARSHALL is fairly considered as entitled to whatever praise or blame is to be had for initiating judicial review in American constitutional law. In the Constitutional Convention conflicting views on the propriety of judicial review were firmly expressed. The convention did not, however, select words which would clearly settle this conflict. The way was open to John Marshall to make the choice.

Since my topic starts with the invocation of judicial review, I may be permitted to add a few words to the millions which have been said or written on this subject. First, I would like to pay my disrespects to the phrase "judicial supremacy." Reference to the American doctrine of judicial supremacy is inaccurate and may be positively harmful.

Each of the three branches of our government—legislative, executive, and judicial—has under the Constitution, as interpreted, the right to look to the Constitution to find its meaning. The first presidential veto (April 6, 1792) was on the basis of constitutionality. President George Washington, disturbed by a bill passed by Congress, asked Randolph, the Attorney General, Madison, and Jefferson to consult and, if they agreed that the bill should be vetoed, to draft an instrument for him to sign. The veto message was accordingly drafted and signed placing the objections squarely upon the interpretation of the Constitution accepted by the President.[1] Since that day, many bills have been vetoed by Presidents on constitutional grounds.

There have been many notable constitutional debates in the halls of Congress, particularly in the early days. These debates have seldom had the aura of deference suggestive of a subordinate body. In later years, there have been at times suggestions reaching Congress that difficult questions of constitutionality are for the Court. Perhaps the most frequently discussed illustration was that of July 5, 1935, when President Roosevelt wrote to a member of the House Ways and Means Committee: "I hope your committee will not permit doubt as to constitutionality, however reasonable, to block the suggested legislation." [2] It is an interesting fact that the suggested legislation was

---

[1] See *The Works of Thomas Jefferson*, ed. by Paul L. Ford (New York, 1904–05), I, 192.

[2] See Edward Corwin, *The President, Office and Powers*, 2d ed. (New York, 1941), p. 279.

passed, the Bituminous Coal Conservation Act of 1935, and was held invalid by the United States Supreme Court in *Carter* v. *Carter Coal Company*.[3] Whether the bill was passed because Congress was willing to leave constitutionality to the Court or because Congress in its good judgment felt that the bill was in accord with the Constitution or whether varied and mingled reasons may have been combined to bring about the passage, I cannot say.

When, like a stalwart safety man on a team, the Court stands as a solid defense ready to meet any difficulty, it may be that desperate problems are fairly left for that defender. If such is ever the case, it certainly ceases to be the case when the safety man sharply limits his area of effort and operates reluctantly in that area.

A determination of unconstitutionality by the Court is very much more conspicuous than such a determination by Congress. Such action by the Court reached a high in drama in the early days of the New Deal. It has again reached a high in drama in the segregation cases, when the eyes of the whole country are turned upon the Court in an acute and difficult problem.

The harm in the words "judicial supremacy" is that in the minds of many they tend to make interpretation of the Constitution primarily the business of the Court and consequently only secondarily the business of others. Since 1936, with a fine regard for what has been well named "political review," the Court has sharply increased its self-restraint. Certainly, under the present doctrines whereby the determination of constitutional issues in many areas is beyond the judicial power and, in other areas, the constitutional issue is to be avoided if possible, the expres-

[3] 298 U.S. 238 (1936).

sion "judicial supremacy" is a poor effort at description.

A distinguished lawyer, judge, and professor at the College of William and Mary, George Wythe, giving one of the early American declarations of judicial review, said that "if the whole legislature . . . should attempt to over-leap the bounds, prescribed to them by the people," he would point to the Constitution and say, "Here is the limit of your authority." [4] Of course, he slipped easily by the question of who was to determine whether the legislature was overleaping the bounds prescribed by the people. Similarly, in *Marbury* v. *Madison*, the real question was what agency was to determine whether the act of Congress was inconsistent with the Constitution. Marshall declared, "It is emphatically the province and duty of the judicial department to say what the law is." [5]

The difficulty, of course, lies in part in the meaning of the word "law." Here law merges into broad national policy. The question may be asked whether we would have had a better policy had Marshall thought that it is em-phatically the duty of the legislature to determine what the law is.

The answer from different people might vary at different times depending on a simple criterion. Judicial review, like many doctrines, is often "sound" when it achieves what the speaker wants and is unsound when it defeats what he wants. When it achieves what he wants, he may look upon it as a great development in the art of government—the establishment of a body of nine men of superior wisdom removed from the pressures of political life. When judicial review reaches the other answer, he may easily consider

[4] *Commonwealth* v. *Caton*, 4 Call (Va.) 5, 8 (1782).
[5] 1 Cranch 137, 177 (1803).

it highly undemocratic to have nine men completely re-moved from the vote of the electorate in a position whereby they may set aside the choice of the elected representatives of the people.

He may go further and espouse a seeming paradox. He may favor a judicial check on legislative action in cases wherein civil liberties are involved but see no place for such a check in economic matters. This may suggest that the Court is more proficient in the former than in the latter. It may suggest further that civil liberties often involve the protection of minorities espousing unpopular causes, whose power at the polls is sharply limited. Whereas, in economic matters, the choice of the people as to the regulation of wealth is on quite a different footing. Perhaps a simpler reason for the apparently ambidextrous attitude of one who likes judicial review for civil liberties and does not like it for economic matters is that he wants an extra safeguard for the former, feeling that liberty lost in the legislative halls or by administrative action may be regained through the Court.

Judicial review has been the darling of those who would maintain federalism, but now it is less effective as a bulwark of the federal system. One may ask: In an atomic age, why should federalism be maintained? What current pur-poses does it serve? You will recall that almost twenty years ago Harold Laski announced that the epoch of federalism was over, assigning among the reasons that it relies upon compacts and compromises which take in-sufficient account of the urgent category of time.[6] Raising the issue of what price speed, one might quote Roscoe

[6] "The Obsolescence of Federalism," *New Republic*, XCVIII (May 3, 1939), 367–369.

Pound saying, "No domain of continental extent has been ruled otherwise than as an autocracy or as a federal state." [7]

I like a statement of Justice Rutledge in his little book *A Declaration of Legal Faith* saying that the federal principle is "rooted in our own experience. It has made this nation great and at the same time, has kept the country democratic. Not perfection of greatness or of democracy, but a continuing process of perfecting both, has been achieved." [8] I hope that the federal system may remain as long as it serves in the continuing process. Our immediate problem, however, is not to weigh the values pro and con of the federal system, but to observe the place of judicial review in its maintenance.

The maintenance of the federal system, as we understand it, involves three types of adjustment: (1) state and state; (2) state and nation involving validity of state action impinging on national power, and (3) nation and state involving the validity of national action impinging on the states. The necessity for judicial review in (1) is clear. In (2), the perils to the national government through invasion of its functions by state action hardly seem to be a present problem. I construe maintenance of federalism, in my topic, to be directed to the maintenance against national action of what are commonly called states' rights.

The effect of judicial review in this area cannot be fully

[7] "Law and Federal Government," *Federalism as a Democratic Process* (New Brunswick, N.J., 1942), p. 23. See on this subject Freund, Sutherland, Howe, and Brown, *Constitutional Law, Cases and Other Problems* (Boston, 1952), pp. 115–117, wherein both Laski and Pound are quoted.

[8] Wiley B. Rutledge, *A Declaration of Legal Faith* (Lawrence, Kan., 1947), p. 74.

measured simply by the number or importance of acts of Congress held invalid. Judicial review may well have a restraining force on Congress, preventing the enactment of statutes deemed of questionable constitutionality. On the other hand, it may have just the opposite result, when Congess feels that difficult questions of constitutionality can be left to the courts. However, the number of acts held invalid may well be of some value, and this provides the simplest measure available.

For the first three-quarters of a century of the nation's history, there were but two cases wherein an act of Congress was held invalid. From 1865 to 1936 inclusive, there were seventy-one cases in which federal statutes were held invalid by the Court, or an average of one a year. Since the constitutional revolution of 1937, I found but three of such cases.

I

The end of the Civil War found, perhaps understandably, the Courts in a strong national mood. The Reconstruction Acts, vetoed by President Andrew Johnson as being unconstitutional, survived Court attacks in *Mississippi* v. *Johnson* [9] and *Georgia* v. *Stanton*.[10] In both cases the Court found itself without jurisdiction, in the former because injunction was sought against acts of executive discretion and in the latter because a political question was involved.

There was an interesting shift so far as states' rights were concerned by the time of *Collector* v. *Day* in 1871,[11]

[9] 4 Wall. 475 (1867).   [10] 6 Wall. 50 (1868).
[11] 11 Wall. 113 (1871).

wherein the Court found that the national income tax could not be collected from a state judge. Reliance was had very simply on the early decisions exempting the national government and its employees from tax by the state. It was declared that the unimpaired existence of government in the one case is as essential as in the other.

The basic fallacy in *Collector* v. *Day* and in cases which followed it, wherein a person was exempted from his personal income tax because of the source of his income, was the failure to recognize the fact that each person can be called upon to help his nation in accord with his peculiar abilities, provided the call is an equal one—that is, one according to a rational classification. We have no hesitancy in calling into the armed forces the young men because they are able to fight, whereas we do not call the old men. We have no hesitancy in imposing a tax on individuals on a graduated basis because of ability to pay. It is not the source of that ability but the fact of that ability which is the basis of the call and the basis of the equality. There is no valid reason why a state judge, a state governor, or a professor in a state university, who is a citizen or resident of the United States, should not bear his fair share of the cost of that citizenship like every other person. There is an obvious implication in this. The income from state and municipal bonds are now subject to federal income taxation so far as constitutional law is concerned. It would be a strange result if there could be extracted from any principle of dual sovereignty an immunity for the wages of money but no such immunity for the wages of men. Of course, I am not recommending that you promptly sell your municipal bonds. I am just saying, do not expect any protection from judicial review. Those bonds have a very sturdy protection from taxation, specifically, Section 103 (a) (1) of the Internal Revenue Code of 1954.

The protections here and elsewhere through political branches are very substantial. First, they lie in the fact that tax exemptions for their securities are very .dear to the several states and that the members of Congress come from the several states and are very much aware of the interest and the needs of their states, as well as of the wishes of the state political organizations. Secondly, any change in the rule as to existing bonds would, apart from any question of constitutional law, result in a devastating fall in the value of such bonds, which would be very harmful to the economy of the country. So the holder of state and municipal obligations can continue to look calmly on their delightful privilege of tax exemption, though the rule of *Collector* v. *Day* has been dead for many years.

The states have thus far received very little protection from judicial review with respect to taxes on their own activities, as, for example, *South Carolina* v. *United States*,[12] wherein the national tax on dealers in intoxicating liquors was sustained as applied to South Carolina. One failure carrying a whisper of possible success in the future is *New York* v. *United States*,[13] wherein the federal excise tax on the sale of bottled mineral water was applied to sales by the state of New York. These sales were in connection with development of a tract of land owned by the state and devoted to recreational facilities, which tract contained a mineral spring. Justice Frankfurter thought that if a state entered into a business customarily carried on by private enterprise, it should bear the costs placed on that business so long as they were not discriminatory.

[12] 199 U.S. 437 (1905).   [13] 326 U.S. 572 (1946).

Chief Justice John Marshall

Five justices agreed that the tax was valid, but four of them were clearly not happy with the idea that all that is needed for validity is a lack of discrimination.

Justice Douglas, with Black concurring, dissented: "A state's project is as much a legitimate governmental activity whether it is traditional, or kin to private enterprises, or conducted for profit." He would accordingly put state activities on a par with national activities with reciprocal tax exemption for each. That has the sound of *Collector* v. *Day* but without the fallacy in that case of determining the character of a citizen's dollar by the character of the paymaster.

I may ask briefly, as appropriate to my topic, if there is any judicial limit, arising out of federalism, on the power of the United States to tax out of existence anything it does not like. There have been notable old failures in using the taxing power for this purpose, such as the Child Labor Tax Case [14] and *United States* v. *Constantine*,[15] but the successes far surpass the failures. You may remember a slogan of the early fight on the tax on yellow oleomargarine, "Shall the bread of the poor be eaten dry?" The answer was, "No, but it shall be eaten looking like it is spread with lard." [16]

Certainly every tax is to some degree a regulation. That is to say, every tax suggests to the taxpayer the desirability of acting in a different fashion, if practicable, whereby the tax may be legally avoided. Every toll bridge suggests the use of a near-by free bridge.

Manifestly, national policy is an important factor in planning all taxation. Apart from such thoughts as may be

[14] 259 U.S. 20 (1922).   [15] 296 U.S. 287 (1935).
[16] See *McCray* v. *U.S.*, 195 U.S. 27 (1904).

70

gleaned from the dicta and dissent in *New York* v. *United States*, and there only with respect to taxes on a state, I find no basis for the idea that this means for carrying out national policy is to be restrained by federalism.

II

There are few instances, as you know, in which acts of Congress were held invalid as going beyond the commerce power. The instances are well known because of their dramatic character.

The commerce power was almost unused by Congress until the nation was one hundred years old. This failure of Congress to act was due in large part, in the early years, to the relatively primitive and isolated condition of the country and in later years to the *laissez-faire* attitude which predominated. To these conventional reasons there may be added with confidence the lobbying of the emerging trusts. Finally, the Wabash Case [17] and the demand for restraint of powerful business combinations helped make action by Congress imperative. Even then, the Court was reticent. The Sherman Anti-Trust Act received a crippling interpretation in the American Sugar Refining Case [18] in 1900. Though the American Sugar Refining Company had acquired "nearly complete control of the manufacture of refined sugar within the United States," the act striking at combinations which monopolized trade in commerce among the several states was not held applicable to this monopoly because the business of sugar refining was thought to bear no direct relation to commerce between the states.

[17] 118 U.S. 557 (1886).
[18] *U.S.* v. *E. C. Knight Co.*, 156 U.S. 1 (1895).

With the beginning of the twentieth century, however, the commerce power of Congress developed a great deal of momentum. Fully effective with the Lottery Case [19] and continuing until the Child Labor [20] decision, a simple principle was applied. The power to regulate interstate commerce includes the power to prohibit, and the impact on state police powers was at first apparently not material. Interstate transportation and travel could be prohibited by Congress to serve its conception of the public good. The recoil came when Congress sought to use this technique to stop child labor. The Court felt that it must find a stopping place lest the position of the states be eliminated. The stopping place chosen was a particularly unfortunate one for many reasons. Not the least of these was the unrealistic argument that when children made goods the evil occurred before interstate commerce began, and thus the interstate commerce was not a party to the evil. Following the Child Labor Case, there was, of course, a period of some eighteen years when the commerce power of Congress was measured substantially by a concept of state power. This effort to find a stopping point to the commerce power of Congress reached its climax in the early days of the New Deal, until the effort was brought to an abrupt end in *National Labor Relations Board v. Jones and Laughlin* [21] and reinforced by *Wickard v. Filburn*.[22] While I would not put it beyond the realm of possibility, it is certainly hard to suppose at this time than any act that Congress passes under the commerce power will be found by the Court to be so little connected with commerce as to be invalid.

[19] 188 U.S. 321 (1903). [20] 247 U.S. 251 (1918).
[21] 301 U.S. 1 (1937). [22] 317 U.S. 111 (1942).

Obviously, the technique of prohibiting movement from state to state as a means of controlling activity within the United States has notable and almost endless possibilities. It would, of course, be checked by the due-process clause and other express limitations in the Constitution. We would not suppose, for example, that Congress could prohibit Republicans from crossing state lines to go home for an election. Could Congress prohibit the passage across state lines of persons seeking the benefits of a divorce law which Congress felt to be too liberal? It has used the taxing power to prevent state competition for the wealthy through the bait of no inheritance tax. Could it use the commerce power to prevent reckless competition for divorce business? However that may be, a limitation on the basis of states' rights seems to be difficult to find.

The logic of the commerce clause is quite simple. The power of Congress to regulate commerce is plenary and extends to all commerce which affects more states than one. Of course, the commercial life of the United States has become so much of one piece that it is difficult to find any economic activity of importance which does not affect more states than one. We have very nearly reached the belief that commerce among the several states means commerce within the area of the several states. Doubtless, in the classroom, students will continue to argue about the bootblack and the barber, but such problems will hardly reach the level of congressional concern.

III

The idea of careful limitations on the province of the judiciary is, of course, as old as the framing of the Con-

stitution. The Founding Fathers considered and rejected
the suggestion of allowing each branch of the legislature,
as well as the President, to require opinions of the Supreme
Court on important questions of law. The constitutional
provision limiting jurisdiction to cases and controversies
has been rigorously followed with much learning on what
is a case or controversy and on such matters as adverse
interests and friendly suits.

Justice Frankfurter said: "The jurisdiction of the federal
Courts can be invoked only under circumstances, which
to the expert feel of lawyers, constitute a case or controversy." [23] The invocation of the "expert feel of lawyers"
gently expresses the fact that the subject defies the rigor of
precise rules and lies largely in the intuitive judgment of
the courts—or, if one prefers, in the Court's sense of wise
policy. This freedom of choice in the judges has been expressed somewhat more critically in the statement "that
cases and controversies, adverse parties, substantial interest,
and real questions are no more than trees behind which
the Judges hide when they wish either to throw stones at
Congress or the President or to escape from those who are
urging them to do so." [24]

The Court early recognized the idea that certain controversies were really beyond the judicial orbit and fell
better within the scope of political branches of the government. Thus in 1848 the Court refused to decide between
two competing state governments.[25]

The very interesting case of *Frothingham* v. *Mellon* [26]

[23] *Joint Anti-Fascist Refugee Committee* v. *McGrath*, 341 U.S.
123, 150 (1951).
[24] Robert J. Harris, *The Judicial Power of the United States* (Baton
Rouge, La., 1940), p. 23. 262 U.S. 447 (1923).
[25] *Luther* v. *Borden*, 7 How. 1.   [26] 262 U.S. 447 (1923).

involves a union or a confusion of the concept of a case or a controversy and that of a political question. In addition, it practically, if not absolutely, freed the spending power from judicial review. Frothingham claimed standing to sue as a taxpayer to enjoin Mellon, the Secretary of the Treasury, from making certain expenditures, on the ground that the expenditures were unconstitutional and hence would improperly increase the burden of future taxation. The Court commented extensively on the minute interest of the individual citizen in the national Treasury since he shared an interest with "millions of others." That his interest was small may be unimportant, since Courts do not exist simply to protect large interests. However, his interest was indistinguishable from that of millions of other fellow citizens. This generality of interest as distinguished from a particularity of interest is relevant not only to the problem of a case or controversy but is a determining factor in what is a political question. An interest which an individual has in common with his fellow citizens constitutes the normal business of legislative and executive branches, for which adequate political checks are available. If the people don't like the kind of laws a legislature is giving them, it is up to them to elect a new legislature. If the majority picks on itself, it has only itself to blame. It is only when the majority picks on the minority that political checks do not avail. In such cases, there may well be a particularity of interest necessary to maintain an action.

The policy reasons for hesitation of the Court to set aside an act of Congress are obvious. The whole machinery of the legislative branch having been put into effect—the investigations of committees, the discussions on the floor of Congress, the vote of the chosen representatives of the people, and the right of the people to show their pleasure or displeasure at the polls—make this an event to be avoided if it can decently be done.

IV

By way of conclusion, it may be well merely to remind you that federalism rests quite securely in the structure of our government. James Madison, in the *Federalist Papers*, No. 46, wrote of the strength of the local spirit to be expected in members of Congress. This local spirit has certainly been apparent in many respects. The members of Congress have often had their early political training in state politics and frequently are closely tied in with a political organization of long standing in their several states. Accordingly, the interests of the states as distinguished from the interests of a mass of people of the United States are likely to get careful attention in the Congress. Furthermore, apart from such practical political considerations as party politics at the state level, there is always the structure of the United States Senate with its two members for every state. It does not take much imagination to recognize the voting power and the bargaining power therein involved for each separate state. The Court is not a guardian of the federal system, which it once was. The Senate, however, has not lost its powers.

VI. John Marshall and the American Judicial Tradition

BY CHARLES FAIRMAN

THERE is a great deal of John Marshall that lives in us all. No doubt many a one is conscious—not only here and now, but at all times—that Marshall is the companion of his thoughts. Every lawyer in America has caught at least something of the great Chief's liberality of principle. Every American judge acknowledges Marshall to be the judicial prototype. In the Supreme Court—the part of government that is longest in its memory and most conscious of its continuity—Marshall's presence is constantly felt. Hence the topic I have chosen: Marshall and our judicial tradition.

"Let it be remembered, that, when Chief Justice Marshall first took his seat on the bench, scarcely more than two or three questions of constitutional law had ever engaged the attention of the Supreme Court." It was

Justice Story who gave that low estimate of what had been accomplished between 1790 and 1801; he was speaking *in memoriam*, before the Suffolk bar, at Boston, in 1835.[1] Go back to the rather unfamiliar pages of 2, 3, and 4 Dallas, where the early cases in the Supreme Court were reported, thinly, along with decisions of the Supreme Court of Pennsylvania and some other courts. That, one sees, was a season of lost opportunities. The justices badly needed direction, purpose, method, a sense of vocation. When Marshall came to the Court it was a time—high time—for greatness. Surely this is once when the impact of a man became itself a force in history. Holmes, sitting on the Massachusetts bench, said, you will remember, that "part of [Marshall's] greatness consists in his being *there*." [2] True, no doubt, but if it had been someone else who was *there*—John Jay, who declined reappointment, or Justice Paterson, whom Federalist leaders favored—would this nation be all that it is today? Suppose the choice had fallen into Jefferson's hands, and the chief justiceship had been given to Spencer Roane—would even an indulgent alma mater arrange a bicentennial celebration here at Williamsburg when 1962 comes around? All this I doubt. We are assembled here today, not merely because of the circumstance that "there fell to Marshall perhaps the greatest place that was ever filled by a judge," [3] but because he filled it with a native greatness that remains a source of strength today.

[1] *The Miscellaneous Writings of Joseph Story*, ed. by W. W. Story (Boston, 1852), pp. 639, 695.

[2] Answer to a motion that the Court adjourn on the one-hundredth anniversary of the day Marshall took his seat as Chief Justice. *Speeches by Oliver Wendell Holmes* (Boston, 1934), pp. 87, 88.

[3] Holmes, *ibid.*, p. 90.

II

"We must never forget that it is a constitution we are expounding." [4] The immediate problem in *McCulloch* v. *Maryland*—the validity of an act of Congress incorporating a bank—lies far behind us; the Court's response is familiar and may now seem a commonplace. "Let the end be legitimate," and the means, plainly adapted, are constitutional. That was no commonplace in 1819. At the close of the term the Chief came home to find that Judge Roane had "aroused the sleeping spirit of Virginia, if indeed it ever sleeps." [5] Marshall, usually so steady, so adequately sustained within himself, took an extraordinary —and false—step. He met the anonymous attacks by an anonymous reply. But Marshall the polemic was sadly inferior to Marshall the Chief Justice. Let us dismiss the episode with the thought of how deeply he was hurt when his neighbors withheld their confidence, how masterful and right he had been in the exercise of his office.

It has never, I believe, been helpful for a justice to resort to extrajudicial protestations. Appeals for vindication are exceptional; austere silence has been the rule. In the end, it is his works that must be a judge's justification—and in the fullness of time they are, according to his merit.

The memorable commotion raised against the McCulloch opinion and its doctrine of implied powers was reflected in Justice Story's address on "Progress in Jurisprudence" before the Suffolk County Bar in 1821:

We have lived to see this constitution, the great bond and bulwark of the Union, subjected to a minute and verbal criticism,

[4] *McCulloch* v. *Maryland*, 4 Wheat. 316, 407 (1819).
[5] Beveridge, *The Life of John Marshall* (Boston, 1919), IV, 312.

which the common law repudiated even in its most rigorous construction of the grants of kings; a criticism, which scarcely belonged to the stinted charter of a petty municipality. Attempts have been made, honestly if you please, but in the spirit of over curious jealousy, to cripple its general powers, by denying the means, when the end is required; to interpret a form of government, necessarily dealing in general expressions, . . . like the grant of a free fishery, or an easement, or franchise against common right; instead of interpreting it as a constitution to regulate great national concerns, and to protect and sustain the citizens against domestic misrule, as well as foreign aggression. Even its enumerated powers have been strained into a forced and unnatural posture, and tied down upon the uneasy bed of Procrustes.[6]

The process of finding the law is a captivating subject for reflection; especially is this true in the peculiar setting of the American Constitution. In any legal system, jurists will differ among themselves in their mode of finding the law. Some will dwell upon the letter, will seek a mechanical rule, not much concerned about larger considerations. Some, of ampler mold, will look to the spirit and the great design—to the reason of the thing, to the ends of justice, to social utility. The Romans, of course, well knew these contrasts. The Digest abounds in texts pointing in various instances to some broader view. Infinitely more important than these particular professions is the fact that largely by the creative work of juris consults the Roman system, through a millennium, kept moving toward a more rational order, a deeper justice, a better response to the evolving needs of a gifted people. And after this mighty movement had run its course, Roman law had a revival

[6] *Miscellaneous Writings of Story*, p. 230.

and entered on a new career in the service of the nations of western Europe.

Our system of the common law has gone through a like development. English law, in the early writings, knew the same sort of generous sentences—e.g., that interpretations should be benignant, in order that a thing may prevail rather than perish.[7] Infinitely more important than these particular expressions of an illumined view, however, is the fact that, largely through the work of the courts, the common law broadened with the needs of the community —it grew in reason, in justice, in utility. "The object of the common law is to solve difficulties and adjust relations in social and commercial life," said Justice McCardie of the King's Bench Division in 1924.[8] (McCardie, I should recall, was a progressive and an articulate judge, in a period when English law was in an expansive mood.) The common law "must grow with the development of the nation," he continued. "An expanding society demands an expanding common law." This, you will recognize, expressed, somewhat exuberantly, the spirit of Lord Mansfield, who in his day—to quote Justice Story—"breathe[d] into our common law an energy suited to the wants, the commercial interests, and the enterprise of the age." [9]

Any state, to be sound and viable, must find its own means for infusing and renewing an energy in its law, in response to the wants, the interests, the enterprise of the people. How was this to be in our "more perfect Union?" Surely in finding the law for the American people, one na-

[7] Bracton, lib. 2, f. 95b; Coke, *Commentary upon Littleton*, 36a.
[8] *Prager* v. *Blatspiel, Stamp* and *Heacock, Ltd.* [1924], 1 K.B. 566, 570.
[9] This was in the course of a memorial of Chief Justice Isaac Parker of Massachusetts. *Miscellaneous Writings of Story*, p. 814.

tion resting on the great constituent act of 1787, there was needed a breadth of principle, a resourcefulness, a sense of high purpose, a mobility far beyond anything thereto-fore known to juristic experience. Those who supposed that the United States could endure on the basis of some mechanical compact, some narrow theory of mere agency, appear in the perspective of history to have been short-sighted and imperceptive. We now say with pride that there had been "called into life a being the development of which could not have been foreseen completely by the most gifted of its begetters"; that "it was enough for them to realize or to hope that they had created an organism; it [took] a century and . . . cost their successors much sweat and blood to prove that they created a nation." You recognize that I have been quoting Justice Holmes, in *Missouri* v. *Holland*.[10] Now and then that old soldier felt moved to sound the bugle—as in this opinion sustain-ing legislation under the Migratory Bird Treaty. How deeply we may regret today that some of his winged words, in excess of what that case required, have been seized upon by men of little faith to scare us within an inch of our lives over the treaty-making power!

On January 19, 1801, when President Adams looked up and said "I believe I must nominate you," and when Marshall, "pleased as well as surprized," merely "bowed in silence,"[11] on that day, we may believe, Marshall was conscious of the bigness of the work at hand. He did not stumble upon greatness. Two observations, I would quote, from Story, who knew him so well. On the one hand, he

[10] 252 U.S. 416, 433 (1920).

[11] *An Autobiographical Sketch of John Marshall,* ed. by John S. Adams (Ann Arbor, 1937), p. 30. Marshall wrote, "Next day I was nominated. . . ." He was nominated on January 20, 1801.

mentioned the Chief's "simplicity of character"—there was about him "an exquisite *naïveté*, which charmed every one, and gave a sweetness to his familiar conversations, approaching to fascination." Yet, said Story, "I am persuaded, that no one ever possessed a more entire sense of his own extraordinary talents and acquirements, than he." [12] Marshall perceived what he was about; the objective stood fairly in his view.

It is a high quality in a judge—especially was it so in one who was to unfold a new Constitution—that he faithfully represent the sound aspirations of the community. Marshall spoke with that authority. In major part, the records of the Constitutional Convention remained unpublished until after his death. The Court in his time was not concerned with historical materials of the sort that latter-day research uncovers. Let us not suppose that Marshall needed as much enlightment as do we in constitutional origins. From active participation in public life, he knew the purpose and the general understanding with which the grand outline had been drawn. He was entitled to reflect, as assured as was Aeneas, in these events "I bore a conspicuous part."

Looking to the authentic values at which the great Chief Justice aimed, I would mention first the *energy* of government. I have recently been reading Marshall's *Life of George Washington*—in its second and greatly improved edition—and have been struck by the recurrence of such phrases as "preserving the authority of the laws," [13] "maintaining the energy of government;" [14] the woeful "imbecility of . . . government" [15] during the War of

---

[12] *Miscellaneous Writings of Story*, pp. 678, 679.
[13] II, 447.   [14] *Ibid.*   [15] *Ibid.*, p. 231.

Independence; "the debility of our federal system" [16] under the Articles of Confederation. Out of his own experience he could declare with authority that a government entrusted with such ample powers as are enumerated in the Constitution, "on the due execution of which the happiness and prosperity of the nation so vitally depends, must also be intrusted with ample means for their execution." [17] Marshall was never a timid, fidgety man; he was not mistrustful of public power.

The government he sought to energize was, of course, that of the new Union, then beset by provincial suspicions and jealousies comparable to those which, a century later, defeated Woodrow Wilson's League of Nations. (We hear echoes of the same sentiments today in regard to the United Nations—which somehow can be viewed as threatening American sovereignty and yet at the same time as demonstrating pitiable weakness in that it fails to make those Russians behave.)

I suggest, in the matter of federal-state relations, that our thinking today should run in terms far more supple than those in which John Marshall and Spencer Roane contended. To Marshall, "the question [was], in truth, a question of supremacy," of removing state-created obstacles to the action of the federal government.[18] Happily, the supremacy of the United States—in law and in our loyalty—is now beyond dispute. Marshall and his contemporaries, in the spirit that dominated legal analysis of their day, had sought black-and-white, all-or-nothing,

[16] *Ibid.*, p. 440.

[17] *McCulloch* v. *Maryland*, 4 Wheat. 316, 408 (1819).

[18] *Ibid.*, 433, 427. It was an uncongenial concession, in *Brown* v. *Maryland*, 12 Wheat. 419, 441 (1827), that in federal relations there may be "intervening colors" that "perplex the understanding."

solutions. We now seek an accommodation, "a practical construction" which will permit both federal and state government "to function with the minimum of interference each with the other." [19] Political entities, we should now realize, are only means for ordering our common life; they have no standing as ends in themselves.

We still hear the cry of "states' rights." Often this expresses a parochialism, a dogmatic and conceptual mode of thought, sincere but outmoded and regressive. More often it is raised by economic interests that know exactly what they want; if tomorrow some boon from the federal government is sought, the same interests can speak with equal fluency the language of high-toned federalism. Let us have done with bandying rationalizations about "states' rights" and "federal centralization." Let us quit acting like juvenile debaters, scoring their little points in argument. Our federal system offers, not one simple choice between national authority and state sovereignty, but rather a wide range of devices. If we would maintain the Constitution "as a continuously operative charter of government"— that was one of Chief Justice Stone's characteristic phrases [20] —we must employ all our imagination and resourcefulness to fashion the arrangements best suited to the problems of our time.

What tragic folly that any of us should spend time in fiddling on such an old string as dogmatic "states' rights" when there are such burning needs all about us!

[19] C. J. Stone, in *New York* v. *United States*, 326 U.S. 572, 589 (1946) and in *Metcalf & Eddy* v. *Mitchell*, 269 U.S. 514, 523, 524 (1926).
[20] *Opp Cotton Mills* v. *Administrator of Wage and Hour Division*, 312 U.S. 126, 145 (1941); *Yakus* v. *United States*, 321 U.S. 414, 424 (1944).

I am thinking particularly of what is needed to make this country safe in its present advanced position in a divided world. I speak of measures on the *civil* and domestic side of national defense. Our uneasy peace, it appears, will be with us indefinitely—barring the outbreak of a war, which God forbid! We are only beginning to search for the adaptations that will be involved—adaptations in government and administration, in finance and industry, in social service, and accordingly in public and private branches of the law. This is not the occasion to go into particulars. I mention it as a very special and very urgent problem in intergovernmental relations. The war power is a national function. But national defense against the menace of nuclear attack involves a combining in harmonious action of the strength of every member. Thanks to the tradition coming down from Marshall, we approach our future with the assurance that, so far as power is concerned, ours is still, as he said, a Constitution "adapted to the various *crises* of human affairs." [21]

The familiar phrase, just quoted, recalls another aspect of the heritage from Marshall: the *adequacy* of the Constitution to all the national exigencies. It was "intended to endure for ages to come." [22] Within the fundamental law, power can be found, adequate to the occasion, commensurate with the necessities. We might, in a venerable phrase from Bracton [23] and Lord Coke,[24] speak of this as construing the instrument *ut res magis valeat quam pereat* —a construction such that the great design may prevail rather than be destroyed. The purpose being clear, the

[21] *McCulloch v. Maryland,* 4 Wheat. 316, 415 (1819).
[22] *Ibid.*   [23] Lib. 2, fo. 95 b.
[24] Coke, *Commentary upon Littleton,* 36a.

means will be supplied. "It is a *constitution* we are expounding." One of the most interesting aspects of our constitutional system is that it looks to the judges, and in particular to our highest Court, to find law on such a cosmic scale. Marshall's thought has become a great first principle. We have come to think of the Constitution as indeed the charter of an indestructible union, a charter from whose terse provisions may be spelled out the strength essential to national preservation.

Of course, we should not doze in that comforting reflection. We should not put off for judicial improvisation what prevision can supply. If measures that need to be taken would involve constitutional amendment, we should proceed steadfastly with that business. But before we rush into any amending, let us take full account that Congresses and Presidents in the future will doubtless be as trustworthy as those of the past, and that the justices will doubtless prove as resourceful and capable as their predecessors. Then if it appears that we really do need to amend, let us strive to do as wisely for the future as the men of 1787 did for us.

What has been said assumes, of course, that it is the judges who have competence to give the law its authentic formulation—yet *Marbury* v. *Madison* [25] has not been mentioned. It is the great cornerstone of the power of the federal judiciary to test the constitutionality of acts of Congress. That rested, however, upon a solid substructure in English and earlier American legal history. Conceding, as one must, the doctrinal importance of that great opinion, I find myself impressed rather by the address with which Marshall turned a ticklish little suit into a

[25] 1 Cranch 137 (1803).

strategic triumph. Without question, the courts must *construe* the acts of Congress—yet statutory construction and constitutional interpretation run so close together that often it is hard to tell, and perhaps even the justices did not distinguish, which operation the Court was performing. Certainly it belongs to the judiciary to test the validity of *executive* action—on that point history was far clearer even than on judicial review of legislation. As administration comes to cover more ground, judicial control of executive action bulks larger in importance. So when we say that ours is a government wherein public power is measured by the reason of the courts, we refer to something much bigger than the holding in *Marbury* v. *Madison*. It is very easy to believe, as Holmes suggested, that "the United States would [not] come to an end if [the Court] lost [its] power to declare an Act of Congress void"; but, as he hastened to say, "the Union would be imperiled if [the Court] could not make that declaration as to the laws of the several States." [26] It took far greater fortitude, we know, for the Court to make its decision in *Martin* v. *Hunter's Lessee* [27] (Marshall recusing) and in *Cohens* v. *Virginia*,[28] where Marshall spoke for the Court—the great decisions sustaining the Supreme Court's appellate jurisdiction over the state courts.

Chancellor James Kent used to read minutely the Supreme Court reports as the bound volumes appeared. On flyleaves and slips of paper he would jot down his comments. Kent's set of the reports from Dallas through Peters has been preserved in the New York State Library, at Albany. For the flavor, I quote in part his comment on

[26] *Speeches by Oliver Wendell Holmes*, p. 102.
[27] 1 Wheat. 304 (1816).   [28] 6 Wheat. 264 (1821).

the opinion in *Cohens* v. *Virginia,* from a memorandum that has been tipped in at the end of his copy of 6 Wheaton:

It is a very clear & masterly Piece of Logic with irresistible conclusions. It shows that the *judicial* is coextensive with the Legislative power of the Union, & that the Government is Supreme as far as the Constitution goes, & as far as the Government is empowered to act, & that the Judicial is bound to decide on *all cases* arising under the Constitution & laws of the Union, whoever may be the Parties to that case—That *Construction* of the Constitution is to be adopted which will consist with the words & promote its general Intention—The U.S. are a *Nation* & *one People* as to all cases & Powers given by the Constitution —Every *principal Power* carries with it all those incidental Powers which are necessary to its complete & effectual Execution.

III

Habitually we divided constitutional law into the powers of government and the safeguards of the individual. Marshall saw far more reason for solicitude over the former than over the latter, so far as the federal government was concerned. If we had been invited here to commemorate that other alumnus, Mr. Jefferson of the Class of 1762, the spirit of the occasion would cause us to dwell upon safeguards against oppression, upon the Bill of Rights. But today belongs to John Marshall. In his biography of Washington—which Jefferson found bad reading—Marshall wrote of the federal Bill of Rights. In some states, you will recall, it had been nip and tuck whether the Constitution of 1787 would be ratified or rejected. In the Massachusetts convention, "in order to remove the doubts, and quiet the apprehensions of gentlemen," [29] it was proposed that the Constitution be ratified, with a recommendation of a bill of rights that would "more effectually guard against an undue administration of the federal government." That was accepted, and the Constitution passed by a narrow squeak. New Hampshire copied from Massachusetts: its convention ratified but likewise urged amendments to "guard against an undue administration of the federal government." [30] With this explanation, I go back to Marshall, and his comment on Jefferson.

Mr. Jefferson . . . seems to have entertained no apprehension from the debility of government; no jealousy of the state sovereignties; and no suspicion of their encroachments. His fears took a different direction, and all his precautions were used to check and limit the exercise of the powers vested in the government of the United States. Neither could he perceive danger to liberty except from that government, and especially from the executive department.[31]

Jefferson, Marshall's account continued, had even wished that ratification would be refused until a bill of rights had been added.

From this opinion, however, in favour of a partial rejection, he is understood to have receded, after seeing the plan pursued by the convention of Massachusetts, and followed by other states; which was to adopt unconditionally, and to annex a recommendation of the amendments which were desired.[32]

[29] *Debates and Proceedings in the Convention of the Commonwealth of Massachusetts, Held in the Year 1788 . . .* (Boston, 1856), pp. 79, 225.

[30] *Misc. Documents and Records Relating to New Hampshire* (1877), X, 20.

[31] John Marshall, *The Life of George Washington* (Philadelphia, 1835), II, 232.   [32] *Ibid.*

The unfolding of the Bill of Rights was the work of other justices, in later periods of the Court. Even so, Marshall's influence need not be absent from our present preoccupation with reconciling individual rights with national security. Marshall knew a great deal about how really to preserve national security. As a young officer he had witnessed the intrigues against General Washington within the Continental Congress and among certain generals in the Army. As a biographer he had reviewed those unworthy episodes. He had seen the weakness that results from a confusing of responsibilities and an undermining of confidence in faithful leadership. In 1797 and 1798, Marshall, the strongest of President Adams' three envoys to the French Republic, had dealt with the sinuous Talleyrand and his devious agents, X, Y, and Z. He was constantly vigilant, skillful, tenacious of the right, a very model for Americans representing their government in a touchy foreign negotiation. Marshall had abundant reason to feel resentful toward the French government that had treated him so shabbily. Yet when, shortly after his return, the Federalist party rushed into the folly of enacting the Alien and Sedition laws, Marshall declared that, had he been in Congress, he would have resisted those measures. He wrote: "I should have opposed them because I think them useless; and because they are calculated to create unnecessary discontents and jealousies at a time when our very existence, as a nation, may depend on our union." [33] As a member of Congress, in January 1800, Marshall broke party lines to cast his vote for the repeal of the Sedition Act. When the worthless James Thomson Callendar was tried at Richmond on an indictment under that act,

[33] Beveridge, II, 577.

Marshall, then Secretary of State, was present and observed with foreboding the outrageous manner in which Justice Samuel Chase conducted the trial. By this bad law, badly administered, the government had brought itself into contempt and scorn, to a degree that this scandalmonger Callendar could never have attained. Marshall knew about wise ways, and foolish ways, for keeping the government strong. In this respect his story seems fresh and meaningful in our own day.

IV

We had claimed for ourselves a "separate and equal station" "among the powers of the earth." How was that station to be maintained? Looking back, it is remarkable to note how sound and right we were, how well founded in principle, despite our want of power. Marshall had a large part in laying out the lines in public law. Prize law was a major subject in the Supreme Court, and some of Marshall's leading opinions were being cited as late as World War I; but I pass that by as not of current importance. The hard-reasoned opinion in *The Schooner Exchange* v. *McFaddon*,[34] in 1812, the great case on the immunity from local jurisdiction of the armed force of a friendly power, became the central point in the consideration, during World War II, of the position of American forces based in friendly foreign countries. Now, within NATO and in other arrangements for our maintaining garrisons overseas, we have negotiated, without insistence upon utmost right, acceptable adjustments between the interests of the sending and those of the receiving governments. But that takes

[34] 7 Cranch 116.

nothing from the merit of Marshall's rigorous exposition of basic principle. The interrelationship between the world community's interest in the security of international engagements and the national interest in the observance of constitutional limitations is a delicate subject, from whichever side it be viewed. In *Foster* v. *Neilson*,[35] Marshall moved through that field with the assurance that comes from straight, disciplined thinking. That is the great explanation of the role of the courts in the application of a treaty, and of the distinction between a self-executing provision and one that requires legislation to become a rule for the court. *American Insurance Co.* v. *Canter* [36] spoke of the national power to acquire foreign territory, and to govern it, with a quiet assurance which President Jefferson had not felt when that question first arose. Today we are enmeshed in a host of problems of international engagements, of executive power in foreign affairs, of the extraterritorial operation of the Constitution and the laws. The simple, rigorous, confident sort of reasoning that Marshall brought to the comparable problems of his own day would lead us safely through ours. With our greater strength in numbers and power, in experience, in formal education today—yes, even conceding that John Marshall had had perhaps six weeks of schooling at William and Mary— it does seem as though we Americans should acquit ourselves better in these matters than we do.

V

Certainly Marshall did more than any other to establish the form and practices of the Supreme Court. By 1835,

[35] 2 Pet. 253 (1829).   [36] 1 Pet. 511 (1828).

when he died, the mold was too firm to be broken. He created the role of the Chief Justice as the leader who gives direction to the Court's endeavors. He is the standard against which all successors are compared. Taney measured up well; Chase rather poorly. The other day I came upon this estimate of Chase by Justice Miller:

He was slow and massive, with a vigorous brain, and I have often said that I know of no one against whom I should undertake to measure myself with more diffidence than Chase. He liked to have his own way: but when he came upon the bench it was admirable to see how quietly and courteously the Court resisted his imperious will, never coming to direct conflict, and he finally had to take the position which he held, that he was the Moderator and presiding officer over the Supreme Court, and not possessed of any more authority than the rest of the Bench chose to give him.[37]

A great Chief Justice must be truly great in spirit— able to keep personal considerations in complete subordination. Chase could never do that: he kept on hankering to be President. The present Chief has recently given a striking and sincere example of personal disinterest.[38] Waite had bigness of heart, but lacked imagination and authority. Justice Miller said, "He is much more anxious to be popular as an amiable, kind hearted man (which he is) than as the dignified and capable head of the greatest court the world ever knew." [39] Waite wanted the "firmness and courage" that the chief justiceship demands. For Marshall's successors since that time, I refer you to some

[37] Newspaper clipping of 1878, among Miller's papers.
[38] *New York Times* (April 16, 1955), p. 1, cols. 2–3.
[39] Charles Fairman, *Mr. Justice Miller and the Supreme Court, 1862–1890* (Cambridge, Mass., 1939), p. 409.

delightful remarks by Justice Frankfurter at Charlottesville, on May 12, 1953 (*Virginia Law Review*, xxxix, 1).

Marshall came to a bench where the justices had been
giving opinions seriatim—as was then, and remains, the
habit of the courts at Westminister. He established the
practice of massing the Court behind one opinion—and in
spite of the efforts of Justice Johnson, the practice remained.
It is, I believe we agree, wise that so far as may be, the
Court's controlling thought be compressed into a single
authentic expression. I have been reading Professor Morgan's *Justice William Johnson* with admiration for the
well-directed effort, the penetration, and the grace with
which he has worked. It seems to me, in the language of
Johnson's day, an elegant book. But significant as Johnson
was, and vigorous as was his mind, I am happy that he did
not manage to defeat the Chief's leadership and authority.
Nor do I admire Johnson's contentiousness or his somewhat
exuberant style of writing.

We have it from William Wirt—once a resident of
Williamsburg, by the way—that at the bar "Marshall's
maxim seems always to have been, 'Aim *at Strength*.' " [40]
So too in his work on the bench: he aimed at what was
strong and controlling. Marshall's mode of composition,
so luminous, so free from excess, established a pattern for
the Court—which theretofore had had no established
type. In the distinction of his style he has never been ex-
celled. Where another might have essayed pamphleteering,
Marshall stuck to the strait traditions of the common
law. Here I quote some phrases from Story, with which
certainly Marshall would have been in accord. "The com-

[40] Kennedy, *Memoirs of the Life of William Wirt* (1860), 76,
quoted in Beveridge, II, 192.

mon law follows out its principles with a closeness and simplicity of reasoning." [41] "Common sense has at all times powerfully counteracted the tendency to undue speculation in the common law." [42] One needs "to guard against the captivations of theory." [43]

Chancellor Kent's comments often went to form, as in this remark on *Osborn* v. *Bank of the United States:* "The opinion of the Chief Justice in this great case is expressed with his customary simplicity & severe & chaste Logic. His lucid mind is displayed in all its glory. It is not involved & perplexed & contradictory & arrogant as it is in the first case reported in this volume." [44] Of course you wonder, what was the first case in this volume? Well, that was *Gibbons* v. *Ogden,* 9 Wheaton 1. You will recall that on the steamboat question, Kent, when Chief Justice of New York, had concluded that the state might go on in the exercise of the licensing power until it came practically in collision with the exercise of some congressional power.[45] Truly, Marshall's opinion, as to exclusive or concurrent power, *was* less simple and more perplexed than was his wont. But neither Kent nor Marshall had seen to the end of that question of concurrent power; it was prudent to leave the matter somewhat fluid. *Gibbons* v. *Ogden,* by the way, was one of the rare cases where an opinion by Marshall enjoyed a ready popular acclaim.

It was generally easier, in Marshall's time, to be simple and unperplexed in analysis than it is for the present Court. The situations then presented were less compli-

[41] *Miscellaneous Writings of Story,* p. 508.

[42] *Ibid.*   [43] *Ibid.,* p. 513.

[44] 9 Wheat. 738 (1824). I quote from his memorandum, now tipped into his copy of the Report, in the New York State Library.

[45] *Livingston and Fulton* v. *Van Ingen,* 9 Johns. 507 (1812).

cated; things were not so interrelated, in government and in life, as they are today. The Court's practices and canons have attained a refinement that would puzzle the great Chief—for a moment—if he came back. But he would catch on quickly, and how his acute mind would respond to the nice questions of Supreme Court jurisdiction!

VI

Toward the end of his life Marshall began to fear that the Constitution would not be so enduring as once he had confidently asserted. A clear expression of that view is found in his letter of December 30, 1827, to Story—the first draft of which is in your library here at the College of William and Mary.[46] "What may follow sets conjecture at defiance. I shall not live to see and bewail the consequences of these furious passions which are breaking loose upon us." The advent of Andrew Jackson and the movement we call Jacksonian democracy filled him with despair. The Court he had held together, with such kindly deference but with such authority, was on the point of breaking up. Wayne succeeded Johnson in 1835; in 1836 Taney became Chief Justice, and Philip Pendleton Barbour came on as a side judge. (Barbour, I recall, attended William and Mary. Years ago, pursuing mementos of justices all around Virginia, I read an account of Barbour's life, by his son and namesake, in the possession of a descendant at Gordonsville. That letter verified the story that Barbour went to Kentucky and practiced law, saved his money, returned to Virginia, and entered the College of William

[46] This draft, and the final copy (somewhat different in expression), are published with the *Autobiographical Sketch*.

and Mary. That seems a somewhat inverted way of getting one's education.) In 1837, the Court was raised to nine, and Catron and McKinley came on the bench, from the West and the new South. Suddenly it was a new and Jacksonian Court.

At Marshall's last term, three constitutional cases remained undecided, by reason of disagreement among the judges. They were *New York* v. *Miln, Briscoe* v. *Bank of Kentucky*, and the Charles River Bridge Case. They are reported in 11 Peters, the first volume of Taney's new Court—and each was decided contrary to the view Marshall had held and over Story's dissent. The decisions were rather strongly inspired by new views. Two now seem quite right, and the Briscoe decision is quite understandable, considering the popular demand for state banks. In conservative circles, a clamor went up—comparable to that raised in 1937.

Chancellor Kent wrote to the expectant Story that the Charles River Bridge decision, by its narrow reading of the franchise, "overthrows a great principle of constitutional morality." Briscoe was "alarming and distressing." [47] Story wrote back:

I think [the Court] will, &, I fear, it must lose, that strong hold of the public confidence which it has hitherto been fortunate enough to secure—when we lost Chief Justice Marshall we lost our great support, & our truest glory.

He had thought seriously of resigning, but had been dissuaded:

I yielded; & am still a Judge, but with no hopes for the future, & with the deepest sense, that all, which for twenty five years I

---

[47] *Life and Letters of Joseph Story*, ed. by W. W. Story (Boston, 1851), II, 270.

have aided in building up, in the doctrines of constitutional law, are to be directly or indirectly overturned; slowly, if not suddenly; by fragments, if not in masses—I cannot, & do not look to the right or the left *for any support of them;* for somehow or other, notwithstanding many general protestations, whenever the strict test comes, every successive ground is yielded; & I find myself alone, the last Relic of the old school—in the midst of the Desolation. Personally my Brethren are kind to me; & I have not the slightest reason to complain of any want of courtesy—or even of confidence— But I feel daily, that I am among them, without any of the cheering influences of former days— In short, I am sick at heart; & now go to the discharge of my judicial duties in the Supreme Court with a firm belief that the future cannot be as the past.[48]

Looking back, the changes in emphasis brought about by Taney's new Court seem, in the main, to have been salutary.

Time after time, as the Court has been infused with the broadening aspirations of the community, old doctrines have been modified; new interpretations, at first unwelcome in some quarters, have been made, and in the fullness of time are seen to have been just and true. Marshall had lived to take counsel of his fears. That has not been a wholesome judicial attitude. Time after time—consistently, it seems to me—strong, fresh impulses have led the Court to sound reinterpretations of the fundamental law, in response to the wants, the interests, the enterprise, and the sense of justice of the people.

"We cannot escape history." Lincoln said that, in his second annual message to Congress. There is strength and comfort, it seems to me, in the reflection that the ever-

[48] Charles Fairman, "The Retirement of Federal Judges," *Harvard Law Review,* LI (1938), 397, 412, 413. The letter is in the New York State Library at Albany.

rolling stream keeps on moving toward a deeper justice and a broader well-being—deeper and broader than was comprehended by even so pure a man as Marshall or such learned men as Story and Kent. In selfless moods one can feel the tendency of our history toward understanding and civic unity, toward truer equality and justice. We find reason for confidence that "the best is yet to be."

VII. The Common Law

and the Constitution

BY JULIUS GOEBEL, JR.

LONG ago, when Captain John Smith did his romancing about Virginia, he laid a spell upon this land, for how else to account for the many legends which have sprung up about the lives and deeds of her great sons? These fables have flourished like the green bay tree which even the chain saws of modern historians have been too dull to fell. I shall discourse about the common law and the Constitution, and, in so doing, I shall lay an ax upon an oft-told myth about John Marshall. The great Chief Justice, so the tale runs, was wont to conclude the delivery of his opinions by remarking, "These seem to me to be the conclusions to which we are conducted by the reason and spirit of the law. Brother Story will furnish the authorities." [1] The implication of this, of course, is that Marshall

[1] The currency of the tale was secured by the popular biography, Allan B. Magruder, *John Marshall* (Boston, 1885), p. 166. Magruder

was not at home in the literature of the law. I propose to show that this was not true. But first I must set out some details about the way the underlying law of our American legal systems came to be established, and what had been the premises of federal jurisprudence prior to Marshall's appointment to the bench.

We must begin with the transplantation of English law to America. This came about in the course of a sort of adversarial proceeding involving the Crown on the one hand and the colonials on the other. The Crown, for purposes of keeping intact an admitted prerogative in respect to the law and lawmaking, sedulously avoided introducing the common law as such into its demesnes. It did, however, set up the law of England as a standard for the several colonies.[2] Nevertheless, because there was no effective police of colonial judicial proceedings at large, there ensued a process of selective imitation and adaptation of English law and, in particular, that important component, the common law.

Colonial lawyers, of course, did not regard this process as one of mere imitation. They were, when it suited their purposes, outspoken devotees of the theory (which had support in some English cases) [3] that wherever an Eng-

---

allegedly had it from living witnesses. See also the variants in the addresses published in John F. Dillon, *John Marshall* (Chicago, 1903), I, 304, 433; II, 116, 477.

[2] Julius Goebel, Jr., and T. Raymond Naughton, *Law Enforcement in Colonial New York* (New York, 1944), pp. 4–5, 12–14; Julius Goebel, Jr., "Ex parte Clio," *Columbia Law Review*, LIV (1954), 460 ff.

[3] *Blankard* v. *Galdy*, Holt K.B. 341; 2 Salkeld 411; 4 Modern 222; Comberbach 228 (1693); *Privy Council Memorandum*, 2 Peere Williams 75 (1722).

lishman goes he carries his law with him, for it is his birth-
right.

This theory of transplantation assumed great importance
in the struggles immediately preceding the Revolution, for
the simple reason that the substance of individual constitutional rights was imbedded in the common law, and
of this the colonials were well aware. This was a fine and
powerful political weapon. Inevitably, the platform of constitutional rights adopted by the First Continental Congress in 1774 embodied the resolve that the colonists were
entitled to the common law of England.[4]

When the revolting colonies set about to reorganize
their frames of government, they undertook to nail down
this claim of right, by statute or by constitutional provision. In some cases (as in New York and Pennsylvania)
these reception provisions affirmed the *status quo*—that is
to say, so much of the common law as had been adopted
was to remain in force. In other cases (as in Maryland and
Virginia) there was a blanket adoption without reservation
as to date or extent. In all cases there was a saving of
colonial legislation. A certain continuity of provincial legal
tradition was thus assured, and at the same time local diversity was preserved. The several American jurisdictions
had each played their own variations upon the manifold
themes of common law substance and procedure. They
were to continue to do so.

In the light of these diversities, it naturally excites one's
interest that in 1787 a reception clause was not deemed
essential to the formation of a more perfect union. The
Constitution was, of course, drawn by men who had the

[4] *Journals of the Continental Congress*, ed. by W. C. Ford (1904),
I, 63.

common law habit of thought and who were lettered in its great bibles, Sir Edward Coke's four *Institutes*, Thomas Wood's *Institute of the Laws of England*, and Blackstone's *Commentaries*. The instrument is well seasoned with condiments from English law—the basic dichotomy of law and equity, jury trial, bills of attainder, habeas corpus, and the like. Yet not even out of the sum of these can a general reception provision be constructed.

In the discussions over the adoption of the Constitution, there were some, and notably George Mason, who deplored the absence of such a provision.[5] But the debates and arguments on the judicial power were concerned primarily with general jurisdiction and with details such as jury trial, the meaning of appeals, and a variety of matter which is conveniently grouped under the concept "due process of law" in its broadest sense. Since 1774 there had been considerable abatement in popular enthusiasm over the common law; in many a legislature there had been determined butchery of our English heritage. What men wanted to salve and safeguard were the guarantees of individual rights; and this is what in the end they effected.

How did the leaders of those times expect the jurisdiction in law and equity of the Constitution to be implemented? The door was open for the Congress to give the

[5] *"Objections of the Hon. George Mason to the Proposed Federal Constitution of the United States,"* reprinted in Paul L. Ford, *Pamphlets on the Constitution* (Brooklyn, N.Y., 1888), p. 329. See also the remarks of Patrick Henry, in Jonathan Elliot, *Debates . . . on the Adoption of the Federal Constitution*, 2d ed. (Philadelphia, 1861), III, 446–447. The reply of Nicholas that inserting a common law reception provision would make it immutable (*ibid.*, p. 451), was reiterated by Randolph (*ibid.*, p. 469). Compare Hamilton's remarks in *The Federalist*, no. 84, and Iredell's tract in Ford, *Pamphlets*, p. 336.

directions, and insofar as any specification of underlying law was made (as the states had done in their reception provisions) this body succeeded in leaving us with plenty of premises but very doubtful conclusions.

The vehicle was the Judiciary Act of 1789.[6] The lavish use of common law terminology—writs, process, issues of law, pleas, demurrers, record, and the like—makes obvious the intent of erecting a system that would resemble *modo et forma* the systems of the thirteen constituents of the new federal union. It is no less apparent that the new judicial establishment was not to be tied to any single model. For on the courts of the United States was conferred power to issue all writs necessary for the exercise of their respective jurisdictions "agreeable to the principles and usages of law." The "usual course" of courts of law was to govern award of new trials; and elsewhere in the statute the same sort of general words appear. Such words did not exclude direct recourse to English forms or substance. It seems probable, however, that a direct transfusion of common law blood was not intended. This may be inferred from Section 34 of the Judiciary Act and from the Process Act enacted five days later.[7]

Section 34 was added in the course of the debate in the Senate. It is the closest Congress came to an outright reception provision—not of English but of American law. It provides: "That the laws of the several states except where the Constitution, treaties or statutes of the United

[6] Act of Sept. 24, 1789, 1 U.S. *Statutes at Large*, 73.

[7] Act of Sept. 29, 1789. 1 U.S. *Statutes at Large*, 93. The subsequent Process Act of 1792 (*ibid.*, 275) had the effect of freezing the forms then adopted. By giving the federal courts the discretion of alteration it set them at liberty to fix their own precedents in this important area.

States shall otherwise require or provide, shall be regarded as rules of decision in trials at common law, in the courts of the United States, in cases where they apply."

The history of how this section was applied in diversity cases and the disputes over what it comprehended have tended to obscure what appears to me to have been the function it was designed to serve in relation to the whole scheme of jurisdictional partition. You will recall, of course, that barring causes criminal, the Judiciary Act was drawn on the principle that original jurisdiction at common law and in equity at both district and circuit levels was to be exercised concurrently with the state courts, even where the United States was plaintiff or petitioner. In the light of this, by Section 34, the underlying law, even in questions arising out of federal statutes, was to be identical whether the cause was initiated, let us say, in the courts of this commonwealth, in the federal district court or the circuit court appointed for the Virginia district. The Process Act, passed at the same session, further evidences the design to use the law of the states as source and guide, by the provision that forms of writs and executions (except style, modes of process, and fees) in suits at common law "shall be the same in each state respectively as are now used or allowed in the supreme courts of the same."

That the framers of the Judiciary Act sought by the expression "laws of the several states" to include the states' respective versions of the common law as well as state statutes was, I think, conclusively demonstrated by the late Charles Warren.[8] Insofar as the new federal establishment was to have a common law upon which to fall back,

[8] Charles Warren, "New Light on the Federal Judiciary Act of 1789," *Harvard Law Review*, XXXVII (1923), 85–88.

it presumably was to get it at second hand, not from the warehouse itself but from some thirteen independent processors and distributors. It is important to notice further that, read literally, the directions of this section are only as to the trial stage of a cause. They are silent as to appellate proceedings, although, of course, review by writ of error would have the effect of confining such proceedings within the boundaries set at trial. There is nothing in these acts of Congress to suggest the design of establishing a discrete federal common law. Nevertheless, the failure to make specific, except in Section 34, what usages and principles were to be available, coupled with the peculiarities of American practice and the way men then thought about the common law, inevitably nudged the judiciary along this uncharted way. This is a matter which has so direct a bearing upon the growth of federal jurisprudence and the manner of Marshall's participation that some account must be taken of it.

The law in the several states had developed peculiarly because in each of them there had long existed a vigorous tradition of local statutory enactment. It was against this legislative background, lavish in extent, and in many particulars utterly different from the English, that the absorption of common law had taken place in colonial times. In areas not invaded by statute, the imitation of English rules and practices grounded on English precedents had been a very close one in many provinces. Simultaneously, there had ensued a most ingenious adaptation of English rules, a selective use of English cases to implement the completely novel enacted law. An example from our unregenerate past may be found in the tricks played with English property law and the resuscitation of moribund rules about villeinage in connection with the institution of slavery. This sort of exercise with the case law stood the bar in very good stead when the Revolution brought in its train drastic legislative innovation.

Two other characteristics of colonial and early state practice must be noticed. In the first place, nowhere were published native precedents available; indeed, the first printed American report did not appear until 1789.[9] For citations, bench and bar alike were cast upon English reports and English texts. As to the peculiarities which developed in every jurisdiction, the deviations from English norms, the legal profession was memory bound. It is reminiscent of practice in medieval England before the manuscript Yearbooks were in considerable circulation. A man had to remember his law and be ready to vouch the record. We have examples of this from John Marshall's career at the bar on the occasions when he made reference to doings in the "old General Court." [10]

In the second place, it was the habit to argue legal points in terms of principle, and not, if I may paraphrase our New York argot, to throw the books at the judge. In some jurisdictions this may to some extent have been induced by the fact that in many colonies the supreme appellate tribunal had consisted of governor and council, a body predominantly lay in composition. I believe, however, that the cause lay deeper; it was the reflection of a profound and often repeated conviction that the common law was a body of principles—something which existed beyond even the cases in which these principles were applied. Every

[9] Ephraim Kirby, *Reports of Cases Adjudged in the Superior Court of the State of Connecticut, 1785–1788* (Litchfield, 1789).

[10] E.g., *Walden's Executors* v. *Payne*, 2 Wash. (Va.) 1, 5 (1794); *Lee* v. *Turberville, ibid.*, 162 (1795)

apprentice who was set by his preceptor to read the gnarled English prose of Coke's *Commentary upon Littleton* had this dinned into his head. Indeed, the very format of the book was such as to sustain this view—the spare and compact text of Littleton, followed by Coke's detailed expositions of rules, his quiddities and quillets, his plethora of citation. If the young student kept heart and mind on his work and didn't fall to weeping as did Joseph Story [11] or run off to play billiards as did James Iredell,[12] he would remember Coke's repeated admonitions that judicial precedents are guides to what the law is, or the proofs of it.[13] The less stalwart who were suckled on Blackstone would find there, too, the same conception that cases do not make law but are only the best evidence of what it is.[14] Lord Mansfield was voicing common opinion when he said in 1774:

The law of England would be a strange science indeed if it were decided upon precedents only. Precedents serve to illustrate principles and give them a fixed certainty. But the law of England, which is exclusive of positive law enacted by statute, depends upon principles and these principles run through all the cases according as the particular circumstances of each have been found to fall within the one or the other of them.[15]

Lord Mansfield's views, although he would have recoiled from the very thought, were peculiarly adapted to the requirements of a society that was putting into legislative

[11] *Life and Letters of Joseph Story*, ed. by W. W. Story (Boston, 1851), I, 74.
[12] John G. McRee, *Life and Correspondence of James Iredell* (New York, 1857), I, 65.
[13] Coke, *Commentary upon Littleton*, 11a, 81b, 115b, 254a.
[14] Blackstone, *Commentaries*, ed. by George Sharswood (Philadelphia, 1862), I, 69–71.
[15] *Jones* v. *Randall*, 1 Cowper 37, 39 (1774). Cf. also *Rust* v. *Cooper*, 2 Cowper 629, 632 (1777).

form some of the libertarian ideas for which a war had just been successfully fought, and that needed to make adjustments with an older order. At the same time, it should be noticed that, by taking a case not to be the law but evidence of it, the door was left open for recourse to English judicial opinions pronounced after the bond with the mother country had been severed.

The attitude which I have described is exemplified in the earliest Virginia state reports which are in a sense prime exhibits. They are such because the break with English traditions, especially as respects pre-Revolutionary acts of Parliaments, was more complete and came sooner here than in any other state, and this chiefly because of the work of the Revisors. These reports are further of peculiar interest because they are a chief source of information about John Marshall as counsel.

To one accustomed to the modern style of a judicial opinion with its text well larded with citations, as if too wanting in juice to be otherwise swallowed, and garnished *sub pede* with columns of bolstering notes, the reports of Bushrod Washington and Daniel Call seem primitive fare indeed. The sparing hand with which John Marshall, the lawyer, dispensed citations has seemed to Beveridge, his biographer, to confirm his opinion that the future Chief Justice had but a meager legal equipment.[16] If Beveridge had examined the reports at large, he would have discovered the very numerous occasions where Marshall's brothers at the bar, Wickham, Lee, Campbell, and others were equally restrained. In these books, furthermore, there is opinion after opinion where the president, Edmund

[16] Albert Beveridge, *Life of John Marshall* (Boston, 1916), I, 174; II, 178.

Pendleton, himself disdains to cite authority, although he could hold his own with the best of the judicial harvesters of precedents.

It is quite apparent, when one inspects these specimens of citationless argument, that counsel is usually laying down one or two propositions of law as premises for what follows. It is easy enough with the use of abridgments like those of Bacon, Comyns, and Viner to pick up the cases from which such principles are derived. But Marshall also on occasion deals out a full hand of cases,[17] and the examples where he distinguishes the cases cited by an adversary indicate his proficiency in this art.[18] He learned law, of course, the way the overwhelming majority of contemporary lawyers learned it—by self-instruction. This was the laborious process of masticating in solitude the tough fare provided by Fitzherbert, Coke, the "compleat" conveyancers, and the like, fare which modern law students, for all their doting professors, would be hard put to ingest. It is as absurd to suppose the total of Marshall's legal lore was that gained in the six weeks he spent under George Wythe as it is to believe that Alexander Hamilton, himself a consummate lawyer, did all his learning in the few months spent between his discharge from the army and his admission to the bar.

In a period of such pronounced regional isolation as that which prevailed in the early days of the Republic, it

[17] E.g., *Bracken v. Visitors of William and Mary*, 1 Call 161 (1790); *Shermer v. Shermer's Executors*, 1 Wash. 266 (1794); *Roy v. Garnett*, 2 Wash. 9 (1794); *Pickett v. Morris, ibid.*, 255 at 270 (1796).

[18] E.g., *Ross v. Poythress*, 1 Wash. 120 (1792); *Brown's Adm. v. Garland, ibid.*, 221 (1793); *Wroe v. Washington, ibid.*, 357 (1794); *Flemings v. Willis*, 2 Call 5 (1799).

was inevitable that a lawyer elevated to the federal bench should carry to his new tasks the ways and outlook of his professional habitat. John Marshall was no exception, and it was his good fortune that, when he came to head the Supreme Court, the bench had already settled into a judicial method closely resembling that with which he was familiar in Virginia. Taking the early Supreme Court opinions at large the disposition to decide in terms of principle, and to eschew the citation of or reliance upon cases, is manifest and even striking in the instances where counsel had come up with a formidable array of specific authority. Even the professor on the Court, Mr. Justice Wilson, held in check the academic penchant for display, giving way to it only in *Chisholm* v. *Georgia*.[19] There appears to me to have been a pronounced reluctance during the first decade to draw analogies from the English cases if it could be avoided.[20] James Iredell alone exhibits an articulate theory respecting dependence upon English common law as underlying law, for the reason that he regarded the common law as it stood at the time of first settlement to be "the ground-work of the laws in every state in the union." [21]

[19] *Chisholm* v. *Georgia*, 2 Dallas (U.S.) 419 at 453 (1793). James Iredell's opinion has the appearance of great learning, but most of it is abstracted from Somers' argument in *The Case of Bankers, State Trials*, ed. by Thomas B. Howell (London, 1816), XIV, 1, 39 (1700).

[20] So the opinions of Blair and Cushing, J.J., in *Chisholm* v. *Georgia, supra* n. 19, at 450 and 466; Iredell in rejecting common law precedents in *Penhallow* v. *Doane's Admins.*, 3 Dallas (U.S.) 54 at 107 (1795); the refusal of the majority to regard the English theory of writs of error in *Wilson* v. *Daniel, ibid.*, 401 (1798); Cushing's opinion in *Fowler* v. *Lindsey, ibid.*, 411 at 414 (1799); Ellsworth in *Turner* v. *Bank of North America*, 4 *ibid.*, 8 (1799).

[21] In his dissent in *Chisholm* v. *Georgia, supra* n. 19. "The only principles of law, then that can be regarded are those common to all the states. I know of none which can affect this case, but those that are derived from what is properly termed 'the common law,' a law

There is some reason to infer that such a view may have been shared, for in exercise of the rule-making power which had been granted in Section 17 of the Judiciary Act, it was announced at August term in 1792 that "the court considers the practice of the courts of the King's Bench and Chancery of England as affording outlines of the practice of this court." [22]

Meanwhile these same judges on circuit, while generally holding fast to principle in civil cases, would sometimes exhibit sentiments similar to those of Mr. Justice Iredell and were even disposed now and then to treat English decisions as binding. They were at their boldest in intimating or actually asserting that, absent specific acts of Congress, men could be prosecuted and convicted for common law crimes.[23] The late Charles Warren has indicated that such jurisdiction may indeed have been conveyed by Section 9 of the Judiciary Act because of the deliberate excision of certain words from the draft bill.[24] The contrary was not decided until 1812 in *United States* v. *Hudson*,[25] but in

---

which I presume is the ground-work of the laws in every State in the Union and which I consider, so far as it is applicable to the peculiar circumstances of the country, and where no special act of Legislature controuls it, to be in force in each State, *as it existed in England (unaltered by any statute) at the time of the first settlement of the country*" (435).   [22] 2 Dallas (U.S.) 413.

[23] Jay's charge to the grand jury (1793) used in the Eastern Circuit in *Correspondence and Public Papers of John Jay*, ed. by Henry P. Johnston (New York, 1890–1893), III, 478–485, Wilson's charge at a special court held for the Middle Circuit and Pennsylvania district (1793) in Francis Wharton, *State Trials of the U.S. during the Administrations of Washington and Adams* (Philadelphia, 1849), pp. 59–66; Iredell's charge to grand jury Southern Circuit North Carolina district (1794) in McCree, *op. cit.*, *supra* n. 12, II, 410–426; *U.S.* v. *Revara*, 2 Dallas (U.S.) 297, 299 note (1793); Wharton, *State Trials*, pp. 90–92 at 92.

[24] *Supra* n. 8.   [25] 7 Cranch (U.S.) 32.

judicial circles a quietus had earlier been put upon the
idea by the opinion which Justice Samuel Chase had delivered at circuit in *United States* v. *Worrall* (1798).[26] Yet
elsewhere the question of a federal common law continued
to be a hotly debated political issue, chiefly because of the
furor over the enforcement of the Sedition Act. The fires
of this were fanned by Madison's report on the Virginia
Resolutions [27] and by the instructions sent by the Virginia
assembly to the commonwealth's senators to oppose legislation which might recognize a federal common law.[28]

It would be rash to suggest that the agitation against a
federal common law, still seething when Marshall became
Chief Justice, had any effect upon his convictions respecting the underlying law of the United States or upon his
dealing with the traditional materials of legal argument
and decision. Much that he did has been attributed to his
highly developed political sense. As respects the matter before us, I believe that he was guided by his convictions as
a lawyer. You are all familiar with his proclivity to cleave as
closely as possible to the words of the Constitution and
acts of Congress, resolving difficulties by the power of his
dialectic. Entertaining such regard for the statutes, the
Judiciary Act of necessity had to serve as Baedeker for
journeys outside the enactments. But it was a guidebook
which did not show the roads clearly. Most importantly,
Marshall and his colleagues took the words of Section 34
literally. They did not regard its mandate respecting state
law as "rules of decision" to govern and so limit the vague

[26] 2 Dallas (U.S.) 384.
[27] In Elliot, *op. cit., supra* n. 5, IV, 546 ff.
[28] Text in Blackstone, *Commentaries*, ed. by St. George Tucker
(Philadelphia, 1803), I, 438–439.

phrases "principles and usages of law," or "course of law," used in other sections of the act. This meant, for example, that in the section relating to process the judges had to draw their own maps as to the direction in which they would travel.

It seems to me probable that this attitude may have been induced by the impeachment trial of Justice Samuel Chase and by what was there said in the arguments on Articles 5 and 6 of the impeachment, respecting the difficulties of ascertaining what in fact the practice of a state might be.[29] It was manifest how easily a federal judge trained in Maryland's version of common law procedure might err when sitting in Virginia, which had its own variants. If the politicians were prepared to impeach for violations of Section 34 (which was Chase's fate), it was obviously prudent to restrict its effect and to use some other formula wherever possible.

The *modus operandi* is indicated by *Ex parte Bollman* (1807),[30] involving a petition for habeas corpus in the Supreme Court under Section 14 of the Judiciary Act. Harper for the petitioner argued inherent power, the definition of which must be found in the common law. Marshall, speaking for the majority, made it clear that the power to award the writ by any federal court must be given by written law. Nevertheless, "for the meaning of the term habeas corpus resort may be had to the common law." [31] He did not at

---

[29] For the articles, Samuel H. Smith and Thomas Lloyd, *Trial of Samuel Chase* (Washington, D.C., 1805), I, 6–7; Chase's answer on these, *ibid.*, pp. 81–89; Randolph's opening, *ibid.*, pp. 120–123; Clark for the managers, *ibid.*, II, 3–5; Lee for the defense, *ibid.*, pp. 106 ff.; Martin for the defense, pp. 229 ff.; Randolph's closing, pp. 468 ff.

[30] 4 Cranch (U.S.) 75.　　　　[31] *Ibid.*, 93–94.

the time explain why he thought such resort proper. But I believe we can deduce what he had in mind from remarks made shortly thereafter in the Circuit Court in the course of certain rulings made during the proceedings against Aaron Burr.

The first and most important were his opening remarks in the elaborate opinion on the motion to exclude certain testimony connecting the absent Burr with the events on Blennerhassett's Island.[32] It was this opinion which fixed the scope of the constitutional definition of treason. The term treason, said Marshall, was a technical term:

> It is used in a very old statute of that country whose language is our language, and whose laws form the substratum of our laws. It is scarcely conceivable that the term was not employed by the framers of our Constitution in the sense which had been affixed to it by those from whom we borrowed it.

Cases alone were not sufficient to fix upon this meaning. Recourse must be had to "those celebrated elementary writers, who have stated the principles of the law, whose statements have received the common approbation of legal men." Then followed his exhaustive and meticulous examination of the state trials and books expounding the bloody doctrines of the English law of treason—an opinion which should dispel forever the myths of the Chief Justice's ineptness in the handling of precedent.

It should be noticed that except for one parenthetical remark by United States Attorney George Hay,[33] neither

[32] David Robertson, *Reports of the Trials of Colonel Aaron Burr* (Philadelphia, 1808), II, 401 ff.

[33] *Ibid.*, p. 15. Randolph for the defense had been arguing that there was no common law of the United States. Hay interrupted, saying the point did not need to be labored. Unquestionably the

prosecution nor defense sought to invoke Section 34 as a bridge into the common law sources. Nevertheless, there was an almost tedious discussion of these, for it was the prosecution's position that such references to common law were essential to explain the words of the Constitution. The defense, on the other hand, which had some embarrassing precedents to cope with, sought to limit the degree to which these murky waters could be fished. Later on in the proceedings, Marshall, in ruling on the process by which Burr should be taken to answer an indictment for misdemeanor, stated explicitly that he did not regard Section 34 to be applicable to criminal prosecutions. It was confined to civil litigation. He settled the process problem by reference to the broadly worded Section 14, which directed process should be agreeable to the "principles and usages of law." This meant, he said, "that generally recognized and long-established law which forms the substratum of the laws of every state." [34]

The inference to be drawn from Marshall's statement respecting Section 34 is that in any and all types of civil litigation in federal courts the laws of the states were to serve as rules of decision. The Supreme Court was not to indicate its views about Section 34 until eighteen years later, when, in *Wayman* v. *Southard* (1825),[35] this section was invoked as a control on process of execution. Marshall adverted to the general opinion of the bar that Section 34

United States as a general government had no common law "though under the state law connected with the judicial act it might be considered as existing to a limited extent."

[34] *Ibid.*, p. 482.

[35] 1 Wheat. (U.S.) 1, 4. Compare the opinion in *U.S. Bank* v. *Halstead, ibid.*, 51, and what Justice Thompson states (p. 56) regarding the meaning of the language of Sec. 14 of the Judiciary Act.

was to furnish "a rule to guide the court to its judgments." But it was only to litigation in court and not to proceedings after judgment that the provisions applied. The section was a recognition of a "principle of universal law that in every forum a contract is governed by the law with a view to which a contract is made." [36]

This odd way of referring to the *lex loci actus* [37] indicates nothing as to how Marshall himself had been dealing with the laws of the several states. Later on in the case, however, he speaks of how, in 1789, Congress had to prepare a judicial system, "not for a consolidated people, but for distinct societies, already possessing distinct systems and accustomed to laws which, though originating in the same great principles, had been variously modified." [38] Here, I believe, is the clue to Marshall's method of harmonizing diversity—why he had so pronounced a preference for statements in terms of principle; why throughout his tenure it is upon the English sources that he places first reliance.

Some years after his elevation to the bench, Marshall twice had occasion at circuit to explain his views regarding the transfer of common law. It was the view then widely

[36] Compare Marshall's defense of diversity jurisdiction at the Virginia Convention (1788) in Elliot, *op. cit., supra* n. 5, III, 556–557, where the same ideas are developed.

[37] Wheaton headnotes: "It is a mere legislative recognition of the principle of universal jurisprudence, as to the operation of the lex loci." Accord, James Kent, *Commentaries on American Law*, 13th ed., ed. by Charles M. Barnes (Boston, 1884), I, 395. The same principle is differently phrased by McLean in *Wheaton v. Peters*, 8 Pet. (U.S.) 591, 658. "When, therefore, a common law right is asserted we must look to the state in which the controversy originated."

[38] 10 Wheat. (U.S.) at 46.

held that the colonists had brought with them to this country so much of common law as was applicable to their situation. "I do not conceive," he said, "that the Revolution would, in any degree, have changed the relations of man to man, or the law which regulated those relations." Pre-Revolutionary English decisions, he asserted, had "all the claim to authority which is allowed to appellate courts" for the reason that, as in the case of Virginia, an appeal lay to the Privy Council which would be governed by decisions of English courts. As for post-Revolutionary English cases, these he believed to be in a different category— a species of pious opinion—the opinions of learned men "expounding a rule by which this country, as well as theirs, professes to be governed." If these were reasonable and conformable to general principle, they were not entirely to be disregarded.[39]

These views, it may be remarked, were such as to render the great corpus of English texts and common law reports available for direct and authoritative reference. Yet Marshall used them most circumspectly. If we exclude the propositions of law laid down by him as principles (the provenance of which the erudite Wheaton occasionally footnoted), we find recurrent the technique of citation to confirm some principle, or alternatively, the citation of a decision as authoritative with the added comment that it accorded with reason and principle.[40] When an English

[39] The reception theory is set out in *Livingston* v. *Jefferson,* 1 Brock. C.C. 203 (1811). The point as to the binding effect of English decisions was earlier made in *Murdock & Co.* v. *Hunter,* 1 Brock. C.C. 135, 141 (1808).

[40] On Marshall's handling of precedent as authority or in relation to principle in common law and equity cases *cf.* the following sampling: *Turner* v. *Fendall,* 1 Cranch (U.S.) 117 (1801); *Hodgson* v.

statute had been substantially re-enacted here, he regarded English decisions interpreting it to be binding.[41] He was capable of writing opinions in which an array of cited authority is examined in the competent and boring fashion so familiar to readers of our contemporary reports.[42] But unlike Brother Story, he was incapable of confecting such compendia of learning as *Town of Pawlet* v. *Clark* [43] or the dissent in *Brown* v. *United States* [44] which glitter in the reports like overdecorated Christmas trees.

That Marshall's use of common law decisions was governed by a belief that they were primarily guides is borne out by his unwillingness to manipulate cases to accomplish ends which lay without the words or intendment of the American statutes or ran counter to American ideas of justice. One of the earliest occasions where this could have

---

Dexter, *ibid.*, 345 (1803); *Graves* and *Barnewall* v. *Boston Marine Ins. Co.*, 2 Cranch (U.S.) 419 (1805); *Corbet* v. *Johnson's Heir*, 1 Brock. C.C. 77 (1805); *Wilson* v. *Codman's Executors*, 3 Cranch (U.S.) 193 (1805); *Harris* v. *Johnston*, *ibid.*, 311 (1806); *Short* v. *Skipwith*, 1 Brock. C.C. 103 (1806); *Calloway* v. *Dobson*, *ibid.*, 119 (1807); *French* v. *Bank of Columbia*, 4 Cranch (U.S.) 141 (1804); *Alexander* v. *Baltimore Ins. Co.*, *ibid.*, 370 (1808); *Tucker* v. *Oxley*, 5 Cranch (U.S.) 34 (1809); *Harrison* v. *Sterz*, *ibid.*, 289 (1809); *Massie* v. *Watts*, 6 Cranch (U.S.) 148 (1810); *Herbert* v. *Wren*, 7 Cranch (U.S.) 370 (1813); *Alston* v. *Munford*, 1 Brock. C.C. 266 (1814); *Griffith* v. *Frazier*, 8 Cranch (U.S.) 9 (1814); *30 Hogsheads of Sugar* v. *Boyle*, 9 Cranch (U.S.) 191 (1815); *Anderson* v. *Wilkins*, 1 Brock. C.C. 456 (1820); *Hopkirk* v. *Page*, 2 Brock. C.C. 20 (1822); *Nankin* v. *Chander*, *ibid.*, 125 (1823).

[41] *Hamilton* v. *Russell*, 1 Cranch (U.S.) 319 (1801); *Hopkirk* v. *Randolph*, 2 Brock. C.C. 132 (1824); *Kirkpatrick* v. *Gibson's Executors*, *ibid.*, 388 (1828).

[42] E.g., *Coolidge* v. *Payson*, 2 Wheat. 66 (1817); *Johnson* v. *Pannel's Heirs*, *ibid.*, 206 (1817).

[43] 9 Cranch (U.S.) 292 (1815).

[44] 8 Cranch (U.S.) 110, 129 (1814).

been done was in *Clarke* v. *Bazadone* (1803),[45] in which counsel sought to justify error to the general court of the Northwest Territory on the basis of the old precedents of error in King's Bench from royal dominions. But the Supreme Court would have none of it because Congress had not authorized it. Similarly, in *United States* v. *Fisher* (1805),[46] although arguments relating to the King's fiscal prerogative had been urged upon the Court, Marshall avoided this easy but dangerous exit and decided the question of the United States' priority over general creditors by a closely reasoned analysis and articulation of federal statutes. Years later, at circuit, in a *scire facias* proceeding on a forfeited recognizance, the attempt was made to have the Court accept the Exchequer theory and practice. Marshall, reviewing the authorities, conceived the discretion of his Court over the disposition of the recognizance to be at common law. He refused, however, to treat such bonds as mere money-getting devices, which, as administered by Exchequer, they most certainly were. He preferred to regard them as an incident of the administration of criminal justice where justice required that the convenience of a person not proven guilty should be considered.[47]

Throughout his career Marshall evinced a marked partiality for English case law that even the increasing availability of state reports did little to remove. The fact that many of the state decisions were themselves gravid with English citations must have presented a constant challenge to examine the sources on which the decisions de-

[45] 1 Cranch (U.S.) 212 (1803).

[46] 2 Cranch (U.S.) 358. And compare the refusal in *Jacob* v. *U.S.*, 1 Brock. C.C. 520 (1821), to consider the prerogative doctrine that statutes not naming the King do not bind the Crown.

[47] *U.S.* v. *Feely*, 1 Brock. C.C. 255 (1813).

pended. Where these professed to expound common law, this would be irresistible. In any event, as we are all aware, it takes generations of appellate reports to produce what our insurance agents call complete coverage, an approximation of which English sources then offered. In two particulars the Supreme Court gave itself a free hand. In the realm of criminal law, the English common law was used as a guide to the meaning of statutory language.[48] After the decision in *Robinson* v. *Campbell* (1818),[49] in which the Court refused to be confined in the matter of remedies by the directions of Section 34, remedies in the courts of the United States were to be "according to the principles of common law and equity as distinguished and defined in that country from which we derive our knowledge of these principles." [50]

Were Marshall and his colleagues aware that the cumulative effect of deciding cases in terms of principle, of relying upon English case law, and of applying to their own decisions the rule of *stare decisis* was the creation of a new species of common law? I think it improbable. To them the common law seems to have been a thing apart—a vast reference library of principles, rules, and cases. This is exemplified in *Wheaton* v. *Peters*,[51] one of the last great cases in which Marshall participated, where McLean, speaking for the majority, reiterated that "there can be no common law of the United States." Perhaps if this had not earlier been a political issue, or if the badge of the common law's origin could have been obliterated, the justices might

[48] As in *U.S.* v. *Burr, supra* n. 32, 50, *U.S.* v. *Palmer*, 3 Wheat. (U.S.) 610, 630 (1818); *U.S.* v. *Smith*, 5 Wheat. (U.S.) 153, 161 (1820).

[49] 3 Wheat. (U.S.) 212 (1818).

[50] Per J. Todd, *ibid.*, at 222.   [51] 8 Pet. (U.S.) 591 (1834).

have been readier to recognize what they were in fact accomplishing by their process of selective adoption. When the Supreme Court was first organized, they might well have cried, misquoting the poet, "Why didst thou make me travel forth without my cloak?" But they set about fashioning one from the old materials and they cut it to an American pattern.

VIII. John Marshall:

Political Economist

BY JOSEPH DORFMAN

UNQUESTIONABLY, the United States Supreme Court is the supreme faculty of political economy of the nation, for its decisions determine which practices shall or shall not be absorbed in the ever-developing American economy. In this sanctioning power lies the Court's creative role, both for the practices and the ideas that become the basis for systematization of men's working views of the economic order. The Supreme Court is guided by the Constitution as the fundamental law, but the vitality of the Constitution depends on the ability of the Courts to apply it to the exigencies of the expanding economy. This depends in turn on the wisdom, the intuition, and the experience of the justices to gauge the strength of the contending forces that a growing economy presents and to strike a balance between them that paves the way for orderly advance.

Our nation was most fortunate in having, at the beginning, justices who possessed statesmanship, wisdom, and knowledge of the economic system. They gave their approval to measures and practices which effectively channeled the growth of the economy.

Chief Justice Marshall initiated that tradition. In view of what the scholars of the law have emphasized in the previous papers, I need say little about the juristic setting in which Marshall's economic ideas got a chance to operate in decisions. We do well to recall the influence on him of the high judicial doctrines of his great teacher, George Wythe, and we should not forget the low state to which the Court had fallen before Marshall came. He wished the Court to forestall the perversion of the Constitution that might otherwise result from the tendency of power to follow property, whether it be concentrated in the few or diffused among the many. His great achievement was to get his colleagues to join him in key decisions which rehabilitated the prestige of the Court on terms consistent with effective power for the federal government.

It would be tempting to discuss Marshall's economics in relation to the great controversy of his day between Thomas Jefferson and Marshall's brother-in-arms, Alexander Hamilton, but this would require a monograph by itself. Let me note in passing, however, that the difference between the Jeffersonians and Hamiltonians, at least as regards working policy, was greater in political than in economic doctrine or aim. Both sides favored commercial expansion in the spirit of the age. They differed on the methods for its achievement. The economic differences were often differences of degree. This is by no means to minimize their very real differences in political and social ideals.

Chief Justice John Marshall

But to return to Marshall. It is as a political economist in a very broad sense that I shall consider him, that is, as one who appreciated that economics was only a part of moral and political philosophy. He viewed economic matters as paramount, for he believed that the Constitution was created primarily to cope effectively with difficulties in foreign and domestic commerce. And he was anxious especially that on great commercial questions the judicial opinions of all parts of the Union should be the same.

Marshall had little formal education in political economy, or for that matter in any subject, but a man who knew the classic treatises in international law, Blackstone's *Commentaries*, Montesquieu's *Spirit of the Laws*, and Wyndham Beawes *Lex Mercatoria* had a solid foundation for economics. He knew the world of commerce and business as did few jurists, then or since. He was involved (as were most men of affairs of his time) in large land dealings. He promoted business corporations in Virginia that were basic for economic expansion—insurance companies, banks, canals, and railroad companies. His legal practice was largely in the field of business contracts. As a member of the Virginia House of Delegates, beginning in 1782, he was confronted with problems of nonpayment of taxes, depreciated currencies, and internal improvements. In the debates in Virginia in 1788 over ratification of the Constitution, he was selected by the supporters to defend the federal taxing powers. Then came his labors for Hamilton's program to restore the public credit. In Congress (1798–1800), Marshall took a prominent part in enacting the first (though short-lived) National Bankruptcy Act and in developing public land policy. As a member of the President's special mission to France in 1797–1798, and as Secretary of State in 1800–1801, he was largely occupied with restrictions on American commerce and the settlement of private debts. With such a background, he could, as a judge, sanction with confidence what became the permanent economic foundations of the country.

Judge Marshall appreciated, and even shared, the business mentality. The successful merchant's mind appealed to him, for these hardheaded people given to "calculations of cold and interested prudence," had a high regard for unadorned facts. "Commercial contracts," he declared in *Rhinelander* v. *Insurance Company of Pennsylvania*,[1] "have but little connection with figurative language, and are seldom rightly expounded by a course of artificial reasoning." An important principle in the laws and usage of merchants, he said in *Edmondston* v. *Drake*,[2] was the "exactness and precision which peculiarly distinguish commercial transactions." Commercial prudence and calculation might counteract aristocratic pride and vanity, and this makes the world more peaceful.

Marshall supported freedom of commerce, but not unrestrained freedom, which might lead to inequity and even the destruction of commerce itself. He was aware that men's passions led them to take advantage of the weaknesses of others and that ambition and avarice were capable of evil as well as good. He favored business expansion for the sake of material development, but he believed that it should proceed on an orderly basis. The spirit of enterprise won his admiration, as shown by his description of the

[1] 4 Cranch 29 (1807).   [2] 5 Pet. 624 (1831).

discovery of America. "After lying concealed for . . . ages," he said in *Worcester v. Georgia*,[3] "the enterprise of Europe, guided by nautical science, conducted some of her adventurous sons into this western world." How little sympathy he had with purely speculative operations was indicated by the fact that it is only in connection with the determining of suitable rewards in salvage cases, as in *Mason v. Ship Blaireau*,[4] that he speaks of a return beyond the "real hazard or labor" employed or more inclusively, beyond the "time, labor and expense involved."

Marshall often used the language of Adam Smith. "Let us buy as cheap and sell as dear as possible. Let commerce go wherever individual, and consequently national interest will carry it." [5] Commerce was mutually beneficial. American commerce, he informed the French authorities in 1798, was in the hands of individuals who conducted it according to their "particular advantage." Consequently, they will endeavor to supply the highest market unless restrained by considerations which make the attempt inadvisable. When the risk of the trade is reduced, the number of suppliers increases and price falls. He felt that the prosperity of America depended on increasing foreign commerce. Our vast, unsettled, rich lands, he wrote, rendered agriculture the most profitable enterprise. The American producer is anxious to exchange the surplus produce of the land for the labor of the manufacturers of Europe. Without profitable markets, their labor would perish in their hands, and that increase of population so

---

[3] 6 Pet. 515 (1832).   [4] 2 Cranch 240 (1804).
[5] "Marshall's Answers to Freeholder's Questions," 1798; reprinted in A. J. Beveridge, *The Life of John Marshall* (Boston, 1916–1919), II, 576.

essential to a young country would sustain a serious check. Thus the right of Americans in common with others to discover and choose the best markets coincide with the just results of free intercourse, for the advantages of commerce were founded "solely upon reciprocal utility."

Marshall's emphasis on commerce was reflected in his view of internal improvements. Along with other Virginians such as Washington, Jefferson, and Madison, he believed that Virginia could become a leading channel of the commerce with Europe. This required canal and road construction to connect the Tidewater area with the Ohio River. Judicious and permanent internal improvements, Marshall agreed, should be the concern of "a paternal legislature," for they "continually disclose new sources of wealth, furnish additional employment for industry, and thus add to the population and strength of a country." [6]

Unquestionably, the greatest service to the economy that the Chief Justice rendered was his sanguine view of the power of Congress to "regulate commerce with foreign nations and among the several states." That power, he held, was the outgrowth of the most serious evils the Constitution was designed to eliminate, namely, the "oppression" of American commerce by foreign powers and the unwise interference of the individual states with the flow of that commerce. In *Gibbons* v. *Ogden*,[7] he voided the New York grant to Livingston and Fulton of a monopoly in

[6] "Memorial of the Charlottesville Convention," in *Journal of the [Virginia] House of Delegates*, 1828, appendix 47. Marshall was a prominent member of the committee which drew up the memorial. Another member was the eminent economist and later president of the College of William and Mary, Thomas R. Dew.

[7] 9 Wheat. 1 (1824).

the use of steamboats on the waters of New York. Marshall contended that the grant interfered with the power of Congress to regulate commerce among the states. Similarly, in *Brown* v. *Maryland*,[8] Marshall voided state barriers as exemplified by a state licensing tax on importers. Those decisions were largely responsible for that internal free trade which few have questioned as one of the sources of the great material development of the United States. To Marshall, "freedom of commerce" flowed from the paramount power of regulation. Consequently, in *Gibbons* v. *Ogden*, he held that licensing under the National Coasting Act gave free passage to boats over the navigable waters of the United States. Similarly, in *Brown* v. *Maryland*, he construed the Federal Tariff Act as granting the importer the right to sell his goods in its original package free of local taxes. The freedom of commerce required positive action, including federal aid to internal improvements, "the veins and arteries of the body politic." Furthermore, an embargo might be essential to protect commerce, though of course a perpetual embargo would be an annihilation, not a regulation of commerce. The question was one of degree.

Similarly, Marshall's "freedom of commerce" did not mean that the states could be deprived of their "police" power, that is, legislation for the protection or preservation of life, health, property, morals, or order.

A good example was *Blackbird Creek Marsh Company* v. *Willson*,[9] a case to which attention was called by Professor (now Justice) Frankfurter. The Delaware Assembly chartered a corporation to build a dam across a navigable creek. Marshall upheld the act on the ground that the

[8] 12 Wheat. 419 (1827). [9] 2 Pet. 245 (1829).

"value of the property on its banks must be enhanced by excluding the water from the marsh, and the health of the inhabitants probably improved."

Finally, in the name of free commerce, the decisions furnished the constitutional basis later for the use of the federal power to curb excesses that accompanied the growth of the economy; for example, such pivotal measures as the Interstate Commerce Act, the anti-trust acts, and the Fair Labor Standards Act.

A basic condition of the expansion of commerce and business was the security of property and credit. In the characteristic Lockean philosophy of that day, Marshall held that the constitutional prohibition of impairment of contracts, derived from the natural right of self-governing men in the primitive state of nature to exchange the surplus produce of their labor. In *Ogden* v. *Saunders* [10] he said, "Individuals do not derive from government their right to contract, but bring that right with them into society. . . . Every man retains [the right] to acquire property, to dispose of [it] according to his . . . judgement, and to pledge himself for a future act." When a government is set up, the right of individual coercion to enforce agreements is surrendered to the government, which assumes the duty to furnish a remedy; however,

the right to regulate contracts, to prescribe rules by which they shall be evidenced, to prohibit such as may be deemed mischievous, is unquestionable. . . . So far as this power has restrained the original right of individuals to bind themselves by contract, it is restrained; but beyond these actual restraints the original power remains unimpaired.

[10] 12 Wheat. 213 (1827).

Marshall held that usury laws do not lead to impairment of contract. Such laws declared that the contract was void in the beginning, for the instrument never became a true contract.

In grave emergencies, such as war, the community may override property rights, for the specific form of property was a matter of convention and law. Emergencies, however, were exceptions.

Marshall strongly opposed state insolvency laws, which he thought provided an easy road to speculative activity at the expense of creditors, destroyed commercial inter-course and credit, sapped the morals of the people, and destroyed the sanctity of private faith. They encouraged the type of businessmen that he deplored. Interestingly, Marshall was overruled by his brother justices on the in-solvency laws. They were more impressed with the need to facilitate the liquidating and rehabilitating process of bankruptcy. But such laxness has resulted, especially through the application of the bankruptcy law to cor-porations as artificial legal persons, that students of the history of bankruptcy law, such as Professor (now Justice) W. O. Douglas, have wondered whether American legis-lators had not leaned too far on the side of leniency for the sake of "letting business men experiment." [11]

Marshall was aware that business expansion required security of assignment and negotiability of contracts. This applied not only to transactions between individuals and firms, but also—and here is Marshall's extension—to charters of incorporation. He provided the basis for the necessary security by assimilating the charters and other

[11] W. O. Douglas, "Bankruptcy," *Encyclopaedia of the Social Sciences*, II, 452.

legislative grants to contracts. He clearly defined this position in speaking for the Court in *Fletcher* v. *Peck*.[12] In 1795 the Georgia legislature had made extensive land grants to four companies which subsequently became known as the Yazoo Companies. They disposed of the lands everywhere, but in 1796 the legislature revoked the grants on the ground that they had been obtained by fraud. Marshall did not question that corruption may have entered into the original grants, but he held that they were contracts; consequently, the legislature could not impair the rights of innocent third parties—purchasers from the companies—without violating the constitutional prohibition of the impairment of contracts by states. Marshall said:

A conveyance obtained by fraud . . . will be set aside, as between the parties; but the rights of third persons, who are purchasers without notice, for a valuable consideration, cannot be disregarded. Titles which, according to every legal test, are perfect, are acquired with that confidence which is inspired by the opinion that the purchaser is safe. [Any concealed defect] of which he had no notice . . . cannot be set up against him. . . . He is innocent. . . . All titles would be insecure, and the intercourse between man and man would be very seriously obstructed, if this principle be overturned.

Marshall implied that the principle applied at least morally to grants by the federal authority as well. Even if Georgia was a "single, unconnected, sovereign power," the validity of its rescinding act might be doubted, he asserted.

In effect, he advocated expansion of the "market overt," where the sale of goods passes a valid title regardless of the seller's authority to sell. He felt it was essential to expand

[12] 6 Cranch 87 (1810).

the area of negotiability, to facilitate the mobility of traffic and of the securities of business concerns. As he said on bills of exchange, in *Hopkirk* v. *Page:* [13]

[They] are transferable, not by force of any statutes but by the custom of merchants. Their transfer is regulated by usage, . . . founded in convenience. . . . It would be extremely inconvenient to separate the evidence of ownership from the bill itself, and . . . there is no usage to justify such a separation.

With this went Marshall's view that negotiability enabled the proprietor to replace at will money invested in a productive fund.

In *Dartmouth College* v. *Woodward,*[14] he specifically expanded property contracts to apply to corporate charters. The case was over the right of the New Hampshire legislature to alter the charter of Dartmouth College in order to set up a new Board of Trustees. To be sure, this involved immediately merely an educational institution, but Marshall had long held the view that the nation was desirous that corporations of various kinds of business should exist and consequently that they should be safeguarded if they were to achieve their beneficial function. He was careful to state that the prohibition against impairments of contracts applied only to contracts which "respect property, or some object of value, and confer rights which may be asserted in a court of justice." Here, too, Marshall implied that the doctrine would hold at least morally in the case of federal charters, when he said that according to the "theory of the British constitution, their parliament is omnipotent" but its annulment of corporate rights might give a "shock to public opinion which that government has chosen to avoid."

[13] 2 Brock. 20 (1822).   [14] 4 Wheat. 518 (1819).

As his biographer, Albert J. Beveridge, has written, the decision stimulated the growth of corporations by placing the security of contract on the broadest basis. By preventing disappointments, it reassured investors in corporation securities and gave confidence and steadiness to the business world.

Marshall had intimated previously that there was nothing to prevent the states from inserting limiting provisions in their grants. Accordingly, in subsequent corporate charters, the states inserted the provision that the charter was subject to amendment, alteration, or repeal, at the pleasure of the legislature. As it worked out in practice, this provision attested to the fact that Marshall's decision had exemplified the dominant temper of the time.

In upholding the constitutionality of the Second Bank of the United States, the Chief Justice supported what he conceived to be a basic instrument to help provide adequate, safe, circulating media and financial facilities. The attempt of Maryland to tax the branches of the Bank out of existence led to his emphatic pronouncement in *McCulloch v. Maryland*,[15] that the "power to tax involves the power to destroy." Since the branches were conceived to be necessary to carry out the federal government's fiscal functions, a state could not tax the Bank's operations and franchises, but the decision, said Marshall, did not extend to a tax paid by the real property of the bank in common with other real property within the state, nor to a tax on the "interest which the citizens of Maryland . . . may hold in this institution, in common with other property of the same description throughout the State."

Marshall recognized the need to safeguard corporations

[15] 4 Wheat. 316 (1819).

and believed that there was no room for laxity on the part of any individual representing the corporations, for such laxity could result in malpractices. He always insisted on reading corporate charters rather strictly, at least when essential powers of government might be endangered. Thus in *Providence Bank* v. *Billings,* [16] where the Court upheld a state tax on the capital stock of its state-chartered banks, Marshall declared that the banking companies could not plead impairment of contracts. So long as their charters did not specifically grant an exemption, the banks were subject to taxation, for this was a most essential power of a state and must be maintained entire. He prophetically noted that a time might come when a duty might be imposed on manufactures. If banking corporations could escape the tax, so might manufactures, and this would seriously cripple the security of the state.

The Chief Justice used English common law, but he used it discriminately. It was no accident that the jurist he admired so greatly was Lord Mansfield, who, as Marshall put it in *Livingston* v. *Jefferson,*[17] did more than any other judge to "remove those technical impediments which grew out of a different state of society." English decisions, however, should be used as a guide only when American circumstances conformed to English situations. For example, there was the question whether the master of an American ship could hypothecate for necessary repairs in an American port without the previous consent of the owner. Marshall declared in *Selden* v. *Hendrickson* [18] that since the same motives existed everywhere for empowering

[16] 4 Pet. 514 (1830). [17] 1 Brock. 177 (1811).
[18] 1 Brock. 396 (1819).

the master to act in the absence of the owner during a voyage the laws of the different nations of Europe on this subject substantially resembled each other. In France, the captain could hypothecate, if the owner did not live in the immediate district where the ship stopped for repairs. In England the situation was modified to meet its particular situation. Since that country was relatively small, the master of an English ship had the power only in a foreign port. In a country as large as the United States, the French usage, said Marshall, was more appropriate; the rule "best adapted to our situation and to the reason of the thing is . . . that the power of the master to hypothecate exists in every port out of the State in which the owner resides, where he has no agent."

The Chief Justice was a hard money man. He favored specie as the standard for circulation and for the settlement of contracts. He was convinced that generally no good could come from the use of inconvertible paper money, which was "always liable to considerable fluctuation." These changes "expose individuals to immense loss, are the sources of ruinous speculations, and destroy all confidence between man and man." His majority decision in *Craig* v. *Missouri* [19]—which declared that small notes issued by the state of Missouri, payable for taxes and other public debts, were void—was no little responsible in holding the country to a specie standard.

Since an expanding business economy required a uniform currency or system of bank notes, Marshall harbored the view that even convertible notes of state-chartered banks might be unconstitutional. His view eventually prevailed when Congress, in 1863, re-established a system

[19] 4 Pet. 410 (1830).

of national bank notes and taxed state bank notes out of existence.

Marshall appreciated that in national emergencies, such as war, there might be a necessity to resort to inconvertible paper money for raising funds and securing an adequate circulating medium. It would be wise to disburse the money with "great caution," he wrote in *The Life of George Washington;* yet the "saving temper of the government, however necessary, might be carried too far," and it was possible to endanger the nation's welfare by a "too rigid economy."

A public debt, Marshall maintained, was not a blessing but might be necessary in times of emergency. The people, even though able to meet a sudden need for taxes, might be so reluctant as to make it desirable for the government to borrow. But the public debt should be paid off. It was for this reason, among others, that he declared emphatically that while the main objective of public land policy must be the encouragement of emigration and settlement— and while those who had undergone the "fatigue and hazard" of improving the land should have pre-emptive rights—the requirement of public revenue must also be taken into account.

Marshall opposed price fixing, as it is usually understood, but he supported some regulatory devices. In discussing the case of Virginia's important staple export, tobacco, he pointed out that its low price was the "perpetual source of dissatisfaction." The best remedy was the state's public inspection and warehousing system. As the "refuse" tobacco was eliminated, the quality of tobacco shipped would be raised and it would obtain a higher price.

"Inspection laws," said the Chief Justice in *Gibbons* v.

Ogden, "form a portion of that immense mass of legislation, which embraces everything within the territory of a
state, not surrendered to the general government; all which
can be most advantageously exercised by the states themselves. Inspection laws, quarantine laws, health laws of
every description, as well as laws for regulating the internal
commerce of a state, and those which respect turnpike
roads, ferries, etc. are component parts of this mass."

There was one decision, *Cathcart* v. *Robinson,*[20] that
bespoke clearly Marshall's view that voluntary agreements
—contracts—were not always equitable. The case involved
a sale of land, part of which the buyer planned to use for
an academy. The buyer refused to make the payment on the
due date, charging, among other things, that the stipulated
price was higher than the "true value" of the property.
The lower court had dismissed this argument on the
familiar ground that the parties must be deemed the best
judges of the value of the property. On an appeal, Marshall, speaking for the Court, drew a distinction between
the price in a freely competitive market and one that
emerges from a negotiation between a buyer and a seller.
This was a distinction carried down from medieval days
and was recognized in the special treatises for the guidance
of merchants. As the well-known *Lex Mercatoria* of Gerard
Malynes said: "Every man knoweth, that in the buying and
selling . . . there is an estimation and price demanded
and agreed upon between both parties, according to a certain equality in the value of things" . . . grounded upon
the commodious use of things. Therefore the seller should
charge according to the "common estimation and course"
revealed by the market. To avoid suspicion of selling un-

[20] 5 Pet. 264 (1831).

justly, the seller should follow these rules: "first, the buyer to be expert in the commodities he buyeth; secondly, that he be not too needy or constrained to buy; and thirdly, that persuasive reasons be omitted, which cause the party to buy dearer."

As Marshall put it in the case at issue, "competent witnesses" testified to the fact that the price had been in excess of the market value. He agreed that such an excess was not sufficient to void the agreement; but if it was associated with other evidence of unfairness, a court of equity might set aside the arrangement. Thus he kept alive the mighty tradition of the "just" or "reasonable" price.

Marshall turned to "competent witnesses" in cases requiring the determination of specie equivalent of payments due under long-term rent contracts which had been negotiated in Virginia's wartime depreciated currency. To take the specie value of the paper at the time of the contract as the measure would be inequitable, he held, for this ignored the fact that the contract embodied in part the different judgments of the parties as to the prospects of a return to specie payments. Instead, he ordered in *Faw* v. *Marsteller* [21] that a jury ascertain what the land was "fairly worth," at the date of contract.

There is no doubt that Marshall had a vision of a developing economy. He was aware of the possibilities of technological advance in agriculture, industry, and transport. Promoting the progress of the useful arts, he declared in *Grant* v. *Raymond*,[22] was to the "interest and policy of every enlightened government." Thus the Constitution pro-

[21] 2 Cranch 10 (1804).   [22] 6 Pet. 218 (1832).

vides that such discoverers should for a limited time have the exclusive right to the use and disposal of their inventions, to compensate them for the "time and labor devoted to these discoveries." It was partly because technological developments could not be foreseen by the Constitution that he felt the interpretation of its clauses must not be too literal. It was on this analogy, too, that he insisted that the Bank of the United States was a most appropriate, even though not absolutely essential, instrument for executing powers specifically enumerated in the Constitution.

Marshall encouraged government investment in "developmental" corporations, such as for banking and internal improvements, but he emphasized that it would be foolish to expect private capital to invest in companies where the government held the "complete direction."

He envisaged the day when manufactures would become important, and he realized that that would entail a dense population, with its accompanying serious problems. The increase in density raised the value of land but threatened to depress the condition of labor. He wrote in 1827: "When population becomes very dense, agriculture alone cannot afford employment for all the inhabitants of the country. The surplus hands must find employment in some other manner. As the supply exceeds the demand, the price of labor will cheapen, until it affords a bare subsistence to the laborer." [23] To overcome the difficulties with which this nation would be confronted, he felt that the country must rely on education.

Marshall recognized the possibilities not only of the business corporation as an instrument for development,

[23] Marshall to C. F. Mercer, April 6, 1827, Boston Public Library.

but also the role of cultural associations. Even a society devoted to the preservation and improvement of the English language was desirable. Marshall said:

At present the intermingling of classes—the intercommunication of well-educated persons with those whose improvement is very limited—the removal from one neighborhood or from one state to another distant neighborhood and another state, the intimate intercourse thus kept up between all ranks, in the different parts of our extensive empire—all contribute to preserve an identity of language throughout the United States which can find no example in other parts of the world. As our population becomes more dense, these causes will diminish in their operation, and without some standard which all will respect and to which all may appeal, it is not probable that our language will escape those casualties and those deteriorations to which all seems to be exposed.[24]

In Marshall's scheme, the elevation of the level of morality was also important, for this was an essential preliminary to changes in long-established legal arrangements which, contrary to "natural law," prevented a good part of the working population from receiving the fruits of their labor.

Finally, no assessment of Marshall can be complete unless it makes place for his unusual psychological gifts. He was a shrewd judge of human motives and rivalries. Behind the calculation and prudence of the merchant, he often espied the mixed passions of vanity, desire for predominance, self-assertion, and combativeness. In the controversy over the recharter of the Second Bank of the United States in 1832, Marshall noted in his private correspondence that

[24] Marshall to W. S. Cardell, June 25, 1821, New York Historical Society.

much of the opposition to the Bank, which had its home office in Philadelphia, came from financial interests in New York. "New York," he wrote to Justice Story, "has sagacity enough to see her interest in putting down the present bank. Her mercantile position gives her . . . a commanding control over the currency and exchanges of the country, if there be no bank of the United States." A recharter might have been granted had influential supporters of the Bank followed Marshall's suggestions to Daniel Webster to permit the proposed charter to "prohibit branches . . . or require the assent of a State to their introduction" or to introduce a "principle which might subject them to State taxation."

There is something to be said for the view that had the Bank been rechartered with modified powers the concentration of financial strength in New York might have been prevented and a future generation might not have found it necessary to establish the Federal Reserve System. And the wisdom and shrewdness of the former Revolutionary War officer could today be useful, especially in the area in which he revealed his talents most effectively, for the problems of foreign and domestic commerce have reached that degree of urgency that had given rise to the immortal Constitution.

Such were the qualities—psychological and intellectual —that enabled Marshall to play a creative role in forging the instrumentalities that facilitated the industrial and business expansion of our country. To catalogue Marshall's economics according to the technical labels of the schools of his day—mercantilism, physiocracy, or *laissez faire*—would be just as foolhardy as to catalogue his politics.

Marshall supported the Federalist party and its successors, and he was unsympathetic to the increasing democratization of political life of which his brother alumnus of the College of William and Mary, Thomas Jefferson, was the spokesman; yet he was not a rigid party man. Northern Federalist leaders found him too independent for orthodoxy. Like the Jeffersonians and Jacksonians, he felt that government interference with the management of private affairs, whether those "affairs are committed to a company or remain under individual direction," was unwise. But Marshall was no doctrinaire. In upholding federal and state regulating powers, in recasting the common law, in encouraging the development of internal improvements by federal, state, and local aid, and in urging the extension of education and voluntary associations, he supported the basic means for the orderly growth of the economy. And among these are also the instruments for preventing those "extremes of wealth and poverty" that Marshall hoped would never disfigure this land as they had England. In the determination of their use in a specific case, the political economist of today is well advised to follow his guiding thought: Experience must confirm what reason suggests.

IX. Marshall and the Commerce

Clause of the Constitution

BY GEORGE L. HASKINS

NO PROVISION of the United States Constitution has been more vitally involved in the development of our national economic life and in the transitions through which our constitutional system has passed than has the commerce clause in Article I. In the third paragraph of Section 8 of that article it is provided: "The Congress shall have power . . . to regulate commerce with foreign nations and among the several States, and with the Indian tribes." It would be difficult to envisage a more vivid panorama of the course of our economic and constitutional development than that revealed in the succession of controversies arising out of the application of this clause to novel problems of commercial intercourse and economic activity. Yet so frequently, and in such varying contexts, has the commerce clause been construed by the courts that attention is drawn to the scope of activities to which it has been applied and diverted, perhaps, from the broad purposes for which it was originally designed and which it serves, and will continue to serve, in the ever-increasing complexities of modern economic life. Because those broad purposes were first enunciated in the Supreme Court by John Marshall, and because his classic exposition thereof has had so enduring an influence, the commerce clause, in certain aspects of its application, is a particularly appropriate subject for presentation in connection with the celebration of the two-hundredth anniversary of his birth.

Of the forty-four constitutional cases that Marshall decided during his term on the Court, three of importance involved the commerce clause.[1] Of these three cases the first and by far the most significant was *Gibbons* v. *Ogden*, which ranks in importance with *Marbury* v. *Madison*,[2] *McCulloch* v. *Maryland*,[3] *and Cohens* v. *Virginia*.[4] *Gibbons* v. *Ogden*, otherwise known as the "Steamboat Case," was decided in the year 1824. The background of that case was the grant to Livingston and Fulton of an exclusive privilege of operating steamboats on the waters of the state of New York during a fixed number of years. Ogden was the assignee of that privilege. Gibbons operated a steamboat between a New Jersey port and New York, and he held a federal coasting license for his vessel under the act of Congress providing for the licensing of coastal vessels.[5] Ogden applied for and obtained in the New York courts an injunction against Gibbons,[6] and the case even-

---

[1] *Gibbons* v. *Ogden*, 9 Wheat. 1 (1824); *Brown* v. *Maryland*, 12 Wheat. 419 (1827); *Willson* v. *The Black-bird Creek Marsh Co.*, 2 Pet. 245 (1829).

[2] 1 Cranch 137 (1803).   [3] 4 Wheat. 316 (1819).
[4] 6 Wheat. 264 (1821).   [5] 1 Stat. 305 (1793).
[6] 9 Johns. 507, 562 (N.Y. 1812).

tually came up on error to the Supreme Court. The question before the Court was whether the commerce clause invalidated the act of a state purporting to grant an exclusive right to navigate the waters of that state. The case was a critical one because several states—New Jersey, Connecticut, and Ohio—had passed retaliatory statutes excluding from their waters any vessel licensed under the Fulton-Livingston monopoly.[7] But the case presented a political aspect also in that it brought into sharp focus the contest between the upholders of states' rights and the believers in a strong federal government.[8]

Two important legal points were involved in *Gibbons* v. *Ogden*. The first was the meaning of the term "commerce" as used in the commerce clause, specifically whether it included "navigation." Although it was contended by counsel for Ogden that "commerce" meant merely "buying and selling," [9] Marshall held that the power to regulate navigation was "as expressly granted as if that term had been added to the word 'commerce.' " [10] And he went on to say that "commerce" not only comprehended every species of commercial intercourse among states and nation but the power to prescribe rules for carrying on that intercourse.[11] The second legal point was whether the power of Congress over commerce invalidated what had here been done by the state of New York. Marshall held that under the commerce clause an act of Congress dealing with the subject matter of the clause is superior to a state

[7] Conn. Sess. Laws 1822, c. 28; Act of Feb. 13, 1811, N.J. Acts 1811, at pp. 298, 299; Act of Feb. 18, 1822, Ohio Sess. Laws, c. 25; Act of May 23, 1822, Ohio Sess. Laws, ch. 2.

[8] Charles Warren, *The Supreme Court in United States History* (Boston, 1937), I, 597.

[9] 9 Wheat. 1 at 189.

[10] *Ibid.*, at 193. [11] *Ibid.*, at 190.

statute inconsistent therewith and dealing with the same subject matter.[12]

It is hardly an exaggeration to say of *Gibbons* v. *Ogden* as does Senator Beveridge,[13] that few events in our history have had a larger and more substantial effect upon the well-being of the American people. But the importance of the decision lies less, perhaps, in the actual holding than it does in the broad view of commerce that permeates the opinion. Marshall saw what the framers of the Constitution recognized and sought to effectuate, that the United States is an economic unit and that commerce—interstate as well as foreign—must be under national and not state control. Herein Marshall undoubtedly owed a substantial debt to Daniel Webster, who argued the case for the appellant. Although we must discount somewhat Webster's statement that, as he spoke, Marshall took in his words "as a baby takes in its mother's milk" [14] and that the opinion of the Court "was little else than a recital of my argument," [15] the impact of the argument is apparent from a comparison thereof with Marshall's decision. Of especial note is the broad perspective, the imaginative awareness of problems, that Webster exhibited. Nothing, he said, is more clear than that the purpose of the commerce clause was to rescue commerce "from the embarrassing and destructive consequences resulting from the legislation of so many different States, and to place it under the protection of a uniform law." [16] He referred to the political situation

[12] *Ibid.*, at 221.

[13] Albert J. Beveridge, *The Life of John Marshall* (Boston, 1919), IV, 446.

[14] Warren, *op. cit., supra* n. 8, I, 603.   [15] *Ibid.*, p. 610.

[16] *Writings and Speeches of Daniel Webster* (Boston, 1903), XI, 9.

at the time of the Constitutional Convention, specifically to the "perpetual jarring and hostility of commercial regulation" that obtained when each state was free to regulate commerce.[17] "It is apparent," he said, "from the prohibitions on the power of the States, that the general concurrent power was not supposed to be left with them." [18] Webster urged that the notion of a general concurrent power over commerce in the states and in Congress was both insidious and dangerous [19] and that the power of Congress over the "high branches" of commerce is exclusive.[20] But he recognized the power of the states to enact regulations which affected commerce only incidentally—for example quarantine laws—which he referred to as "rather regulations of police than of commerce." [21] This distinction Marshall adverts to in the opinion, and later he made it the basis of his decision in a second important commerce clause case, *Willson* v. *The Black-bird Creek Marsh Co.*[22]

The broad interpretation of the commerce power, advocated by Webster and enunciated by Marshall, was to a substantial degree consonant with the purposes of the framers of the Constitution. History, in this instance at least, was on Webster's side. It is impossible to read the correspondence of Madison, Hamilton, Mason, and others without perceiving the imperative necessity that they felt of committing the regulation of trade and commerce to a single national authority. A letter from Madison to Monroe, for example, written in 1785 makes the point particularly clear. There he writes that "it surely is neces-

[17] *Ibid.*
[18] *Ibid.*, p. 11.
[19] *Ibid.*, p. 13.
[20] *Ibid.*, p. 15.
[21] *Ibid.*, p. 14.
[22] 2 Pet. 245 (1829).

sary to lodge the power [of regulating trade] where trade can be regulated with effect; and experience has confirmed what reason foresaw, that it can never be so regulated by the States acting in their separate capacities." [23] The same subject recurs frequently in the debates in the Congress of the Confederation, as well as in the legislatures of the several states from 1783 to 1787. For example, in Madison's notes for the Constitutional Convention we find his statement that trespasses of the states on the rights of each other "are alarming symptoms. . . . The practice of many States in restricting the commercial intercourse with other States . . . is certainly adverse to the spirit of the Union, and tends to beget retaliating regulations . . . destructive of the general harmony." [24] Long afterward, in referring to navigation laws of the states that treated other citizens as aliens, Madison commented on the "rival, conflicting and angry regulations" engendered by the want of a general power over commerce.[25] Early interstate compacts [26]—as well as the Virginia Resolution, which resulted in the calling of the Annapolis Convention in 1786 [27]—are proof of the general and public attention which the problem of commerce regulation attracted. Although at the time the Constitution was adopted the great preponderance of American commerce problems were those connected with foreign trade,[28] it is significant, and indicative of the wis-

[23] *Letters and Other Writings of James Madison* (Philadelphia, 1865), I, 170.

[24] *Ibid.*, I, 321.

[25] *Papers of James Madison* (Washington, D.C., 1840), II, 711, 712.

[26] E.g., for the regulation of the navigation of the Potomac. *Ibid.*, II, 696.

[27] *Ibid.*, II, 695, 697–698.

[28] John Randolph once said that the United States government

dom of the framers of the Constitution, that a formula broad enough to permit the regulation of all trade was agreed upon.

The foregoing statements of Madison make it clear that commercial rivalry and retaliatory action between the several states afforded the basis of the recognition of a need of making a broad grant of power to the federal government and that without such a grant the regulation of commerce by the states would have presented an ever-present threat to the permanence of the new republic. But the conclusion that the framers of the Constitution believed that the mere grant of the commerce power to Congress dislodged state power is supported at most by negative evidence only. It is to Marshall's decision in *Gibbons* v. *Ogden* that we owe the articulation of the doctrine, which has since become basic in constitutional law, that the commerce clause gives the Supreme Court power to place limits on state authority. This is what makes *Gibbons* v. *Ogden* Marshall's most profound and statesmanlike opinion. Justice Frankfurter has said that when Marshall was called upon to apply the commerce clause, "he had available no fund of mature or coherent speculation regarding its implications." [29] He had, however, rendered an opinion four years previously while on circuit at Richmond and had there asserted emphatically the broad powers of Con-

---

"grew out of the necessity . . . of some general power, capable of regulating foreign commerce." Hugh A. Garland, *Life of John Randolph* (New York, 1851), II, 205.

[29] Felix Frankfurter, *The Commerce Clause* (Chapel Hill, 1937), p. 12. It is curious that so few commerce questions found their way into the courts in the early part of the nineteenth century. Even so important a constitutional issue as the protective tariff, which was readily susceptible of being brought to the test of litigation, was never carried into court at all.

gress over commerce.[30] Undoubtedly, the need of a strong, central government was for him "the deepest article of his political faith." [31] Experience of men and affairs reinforced this conviction, for "his mind carried a hardheaded appreciation of the complexities of government, particularly in a federal system." [32]

The practical effects of *Gibbons* v. *Ogden* were enormous. In the first place, it was a popular opinion—probably the only popular decision Marshall rendered—for he had stricken down a monopoly, and this is the feature of the decision chiefly emphasized by contemporary newspaper correspondents. But there were other practical effects which were not only immediate but more extensive. Steamboat navigation of American waters increased suddenly and at an incredible rate.[33] The opening of the Hudson River and Long Island Sound to the free passage of steamboats gave immediate impetus to the growth of New York as a commercial center,[34] while New England manufacturing was given new life because the transportation of anthracite coal became cheap and easy.[35] From a less immediate standpoint, *Gibbons* v. *Ogden* was the needed guarantee that interstate rail, telephone and telegraph, oil and gas pipe lines might be built across state lines without the threat of local interference from state ac-

[30] *The Brig Wilson* v. *U.S.*, 1 Brock. 423, 431 (C.C.D. Va. 1820). It is surprising that neither Webster nor his associate William Wirt made any reference in their arguments to this case which would have strengthened their position.

[31] Frankfurter, *op. cit., supra* n. 29, p. 14.   [32] *Ibid.*

[33] B. H. Meyer–C. E. Macgill, *History of Transportation in the United States* (Washington, D.C., 1917), pp. 107. 108, Table 21.

[34] Warren, *op. cit., supra* n. 8, I, 616.

[35] Charles Warren, *A History of the American Bar* (Boston, 1913), p. 396.

tion. In short, Marshall's opinion was what the late Charles Warren termed the "emancipation proclamation of American commerce." [36]

The political effect of Marshall's decision was, at the time, at least as potent as its economic effect. The underlying premise as to the scope of federal commerce power represented a radical departure from many contemporary views, for example, those expressed by President Monroe in his veto of the Cumberland Road Act in 1822.[37] The decision filled Jefferson, an old man of eighty-two, with horror,[38] and the audacious doctrine there proclaimed created great alarm in the South because of its possible applicability to commerce in slaves.[39] At the same time, the decision marked another step in the broad construction of federal powers, and it became a potent "weapon in the hands of those statesmen who favored projects requiring the extension of Federal authority." [40] Marshall had never unlearned the nationalism he had learned from Washington, and one of his enduring contributions lies in his having helped to educate the public mind to a "spacious view" of the Constitution,[41] thereby furthering the idea that though we are a federation of states we are also a nation.[42]

The economic and political consequences of *Gibbons* v. *Ogden* must not be permitted to distract attention from the importance of that decision in the development of constitutional doctrine. For all the statecraft reflected in the opinion, the case is particularly significant because it

[36] Warren, *op. cit., supra* n. 8, I, 616.
[37] George W. Wickersham, "Federal Control of Interstate Commerce," *Harvard Law Review*, XXIII (1910), 241, 243.
[38] Warren, *op. cit., supra* n. 8, I, 620.   [39] *Ibid.*, pp. 621 ff.
[40] *Ibid.*, p. 616.   [41] Frankfurter, *op. cit., supra* n. 29, p. 44.
[42] *Ibid.*, pp. 18–19.

illustrates the greatness of Marshall's work as a judge. Marshall was not content to strike down the New York monopoly on the ground of collision with the Federal Coasting Act. He was aware of how a decision may serve as the beginning of the doctrinal process, and he purposely opened up certain of the broader issues which the constitutional question before him implied. But he was conscious of the limitations which concrete situations impose upon doctrine, and these issues, though adumbrated in dicta, were left open by the decision. Did it follow, for example, because congressional acts could override a state regulation of commerce, that the power to regulate commerce is exclusively in Congress, so that state laws cannot constitutionally have any application to interstate transactions or shipments? Or did it follow that, until Congress enacts legislation, the states are free to regulate interstate commerce until there is an inconsistent exercise of Federal power? Although adverting to the relation of the commerce clause to the reserved power of the states, Marshall was wary of committing himself to a doctrine of exclusive power. He was even more unwilling to adopt a theory of concurrent power, under which the way would be open for the creation of those conflicting and retaliatory state regulations which he held it was a principal object of the Constitution to make impossible.

Five years later, faced with a different factual situation in another commerce clause case—*Willson* v. *The Blackbird Marsh Co.*[43]—he recognized the right of state laws to operate on interstate commerce matters, but he placed that right upon a different footing. In that case the Court held that a dam constructed under state authority could validly

[43] 2 Pet. 245 (1829).

close a stream to interstate commerce because erected to protect health by draining of marshes. Although denying the power of a state to regulate interstate commerce, Marshall there held that a state law enacted in the exercise of the state's police powers might validly operate on interstate commerce transactions since this was not a regulation of the commerce itself and hence not an invasion of the field granted to Congress. Hence the state law, he said, was not "repugnant to the power to regulate commerce in its dormant state." [44]

From a practical standpoint, the test that Marshall sought to establish through a distinction between different kinds of powers may be viewed as merely verbal, since the same legislative language can accomplish the same practical results. The sameness of these results cannot be obscured by differing labels. Furthermore, commercial legislation and police legislation are not separate, much less abstract, processes, and in concrete situations differentiation is frequently impossible to achieve. Hence Marshall's distinction between types of power resulted, in the hands of less able judges, in a mass of artificial and arbitrary distinctions which are with us to this day. But despite Marshall's formulation in terms of commerce versus police power, it seems reasonably clear that he recognized that, though commerce must be regulated by Congress, local interests pressed for and required recognition. In his own words, the "circumstances of the case" dictated the decision.[45] In Marshall's time, national problems were not seen in the same terms that they are today because economic relationships were less interdependent and certainly less complex than they subsequently became. State legislation, though it had

[44] *Ibid.*, p. 252.   [45] *Ibid.*

woven sporadic networks about interstate commerce, was not seen to affect national commerce except in terms of its practical effects. Hence it was possible to look to the purposes of state legislation in order to determine its validity and to find that a particular domain of state activity was primarily a matter of police power. On this basis, the Black-bird Marsh Case can be reconciled with *Gibbons* v. *Ogden*. In both cases the concrete elements of the situation were the basis of the decision, and in the Black-bird Case, it should be noted, there was but little likelihood of the kind of retaliatory state action which was so important a feature of the Ogden Case.

It has been suggested [46] that Marshall would probably have agreed with the statement of Justice Holmes in *Swift* v. *United States* [47] that commerce "is not a technical legal conception, but a practical one, drawn from the course of business." [48] Probably he would not have formulated the idea in those terms. Yet Marshall understood the organic relationships of commercial transactions, and it is unfortunate that his insights were insufficiently expressed to guide the formulation of coherent doctrine. It is even more unfortunate that his decisions were so readily interpreted as laying down a mechanical distinction between "commerce" as opposed to "police" regulations, each confined within sharply separated areas of power. It was not until the case of *Cooley* v. *Board of Wardens*,[49] in 1851, that the Court articulated a new test in terms of

[46] Frankfurter, *op. cit., supra* n. 29, p. 42.
[47] 196 U.S. 375 (1905).
[48] *Ibid.*, p. 398. Cf. *U.S.* v. *South-Eastern Underwriters Assn.*, 322 U.S. 533, 547 (1944).
[49] 12 How. 299 (1851).

"all the circumstances of the case" and their relation to the effects on national commerce. In that case a state regulation requiring a vessel entering a harbor to have a pilot was upheld as a valid regulation of commerce by holding that there was a concurrent power in the states—in the absence of congressional action—to regulate matters of "local" as opposed to "national" concern. Marshall's distinction thus went into temporary eclipse.[50] The difficulties of determining what is national or local soon became apparent, however, particularly with the expansion and growing interdependence of the economy, and ultimately the courts reverted to Marshall's distinction between commerce regulations and police measures which affect commerce only incidentally. But the application of the test was not expressed, as Marshall expressed it, in terms of an abstract determination of the particular governmental power exerted, but in terms of whether the regulation imposes an undue "burden" upon interstate commerce in the light of the facts. Thus, while a state statute restricting the speed of trains at crossings was first upheld as only incidentally affecting interstate commerce,[51] the same statute was subsequently held invalid upon a showing of its burdensome effects upon the actual operations of interstate trains.[52] Today the test has been broadened in the sense that the Court tends to balance uniformity versus locality

[50] F. D. G. Ribble, *State and National Power over Commerce* (New York, 1937), p. 73.

[51] *Southern Railway Co. v. King*, 217 U.S. 524 (1910).

[52] *Seaboard Air Line Railway v. Blackwell*, 244 U.S. 310 (1917). This case distinguished *Southern Railway Co. v. King, supra* n. 51, on the ground that the latter case "went off on a question of pleading." *Ibid.*, at 315. But cf. dissenting opinion, *ibid.*, at 316.

and to inquire "whether the state interest is outweighed by a national interest in the unhampered operation of interstate commerce." [53]

Looking back over the past 130 years of decisions under the commerce clause, we can, I think, say that that clause has been treated by the Court, on the one hand, as providing a source of federal power and, on the other, as imposing a restriction upon the powers of the states. It was with the latter aspect of the commerce clause that Marshall was primarily concerned, and indeed it was with that aspect with which the courts were almost exclusively concerned throughout the nineteenth century, until, after the enactment of the Commerce Act in 1887 and the Sherman Act in 1890, the federal government began to exercise its power on a scale that challenged important litigation.[54] From that time until the 1940's, questions involving the commerce clause as a source of federal power were the principal questions that came before the Court, and the important issues raised tended to fall generally under two headings: (1) For what purposes may the federal commerce power be exercised, and to what extent, if any, does the exercise of the power place a limitation upon it? (2) In regulating commerce, may Congress extend its prohibition to acts and matters which do not themselves constitute such commerce or form a part of it? Questions included in the first of the two classifications were raised by such statutes as the Anti-Lottery Act, the Pure Food and Drug Act, and the National Motor Vehicle Theft Act. These statutes, of course,

---

[53] *California* v. *Zook*, 336 U.S. 725, 728, (1949). Cf. *Southern Pacific Co.* v. *Arizona*, 325 U.S. 761, 767 (1945); *Cities Service Gas Co.* v. *Peerless Oil & Gas Co.*, 340 U.S. 179, 186–187 (1950).
[54] *Wickard* v. *Filburn*, 317 U.S. 111, 121–124 (1942).

involved interstate commerce, but the imposition of the regulation was for the purpose of promoting some supposed social good, such as public health or morals, rather than to increase the flow, or advance the interests, of commerce. Such legislation has therefore been subjected to continuing attack, first, on the basis of Marshall's theory that the nature of a governmental power must be determined by the object for which it is exercised, and, second, on the basis of his statements that the original purpose of the commerce clause was to protect commerce from state interference. Both of these bases of attack have been repeatedly repudiated by the Supreme Court.[55]

Although Marshall's legal distinctions have been less significant in this area of the scope of federal power than elsewhere, his thinking with respect to the furtherance of nationwide trade by removing state lines as impediments to intercourse between the states has had a pronounced and continuing influence on Supreme Court decisions.[56] In 1944 in *United States* v. *South-Eastern Underwriters Association*,[57] for example, the Court adopted Marshall's description of commerce announced in *Gibbons* v. *Ogden* and went on to state that the purpose of the commerce

[55] E.g., *Brooks* v. *U.S.*, 267 U.S. 432, 436–437 (1925), where Chief Justice Taft states that the powers granted Congress within their limits may be employed for the same objective as the national police power.

The second contention has been repudiated in repeated statements that the power to regulate is not merely a power to promote or liberate the thing regulated but to restrict and control it. See generally Ribble, *op. cit.*, *supra* n. 50, at 171 ff.

[56] E.g., *Wickard* v. *Filburn*, *supra* n. 54; *Memphis Steam Laundry Cleaner, Inc.* v. *Stone*, 342 U.S. 389, 395 (1952); *U.S.* v. *South-Eastern Underwriters Assn.*, 322 U.S. 533, 550–551 (1944).

[57] 322 U.S. 533 (1944).

clause was not confined to empowering Congress with the negative authority to legislate against state regulations inimical to the national interest:

The power granted to Congress is a positive power. It is the power to legislate concerning transactions which, reaching across state boundaries, affect the people of more states than one;—to govern affairs which the individual states, with their limited territorial jurisdictions, are not fully capable of governing. This federal power to determine the rules of intercourse across state lines was essential to weld a loose confederacy into a single, indivisible Nation; its continued existence is equally essential to the welfare of that Nation.[58]

It was the development of transportation and the growing interrelations of all sectors of the economy that brought to the fore, at the end of the last century, the question of how far federal power to regulate commerce extends and what its limits are. At the same time, the expansion of a nationwide market continued to raise in new form the old problem of rivalry between the states and of national restrictions upon state power. Since the mid-1940's, these questions, rather than the scope of federal power, have provided the basis of most of the controversies involving the commerce clause. Thus the aspect of the commerce clause with which Marshall was concerned in *Gibbons* v. *Ogden* continued, and still continues, to present vital constitutional questions. In the resolution of such questions, Marshall's influence has a vitality of which we have not yet witnessed the end.

In this short paper it is impossible to do more than advert briefly to the type of question that continues to

[58] *Ibid.*, p. 552.

arise and in which Marshall's influence is plain. Take, for example, *Baldwin* v. *Seelig*,[59] involving the validity of a New York statute that prohibited the sale of milk bought outside the state unless the producer had been paid the same price as that required within the state. Justice Cardozo held the statute invalid on the ground that such a statute opens the door to those very rivalries and reprisals meant to be avoided by the commerce clause.[60] Again, in *Southern Pacific Co.* v. *Arizona*[61]—a case involving the validity of a state statute restricting the length of trains—the Court asserted unequivocably its function of checking the states in the maintenance of the federal system. Chief Justice Stone, speaking for the Court, stated that between the extremes of whether a state may or may not interfere with interstate commerce lies an area where the reconciliation of the conflicting claims of state and national power is to be attained only by some "appraisal and accommodation of the competing demands of the state and national interests involved."[62] Notice, here, that although pragmatic tests are adopted in lieu of the judicial boundaries Marshall sought to establish between state and congressional action, Marshall's underlying principle is upheld: to maintain the federal system the Court is the final arbiter of the validity of state laws, even in the absence of congressional action.

In this area of limitations imposed by the commerce clause upon state power no more prolific source of litigation has arisen than in connection with the power to tax. Here the problem is less one of preventing retaliatory state action than in furthering, at the expense of residual state

[59] 294 U.S. 511 (1935).   [60] *Ibid.*, p. 522 ff.
[61] 325 U.S. 761 (1945).   [62] *Ibid.*, p. 769.

power, the unified national objectives contemplated by en-
trusting the commerce power to Congress. At the outset, in
considering this problem, we must turn back to the starting
point that Marshall provided, not in *Gibbons* v. *Ogden* or
in the Black-bird Case, but in *Brown* v. *Maryland*,[63] which
is the third, though chronologically the second, of his
commerce clause decisions. In *Brown* v. *Maryland*, decided
in 1827, Marshall stated that the doctrine of *McCulloch*
v. *Maryland*[64] was applicable to state taxation of interstate commerce, and he all but held that the commerce
clause impliedly prohibits *all* taxation of interstate commerce. This doctrine of Marshall's runs like a red thread
throughout the cases dealing with state taxation, and the
underlying principle to which the Court has sought to give
effect is that the states have no power to withhold, or unduly to burden, the privilege of engaging in interstate commerce.[65] At the same time, it has been recognized that
the power of the states to tax in order to maintain their
governments must not be unduly curtailed and that interstate commerce must pay its way.[66] Hence there has arisen
in the field of taxation the same problem of accommodating
state and national interests with which Marshall was concerned in the Ogden and Black-bird cases, and the Court
has repeatedly recognized the relevance of those cases to
the problem of state taxation.[67]

[63] 12 Wheat. 419 (1827).   [64] 4 Wheat. 316 (1819).

[65] E.g., *Memphis Steam Laundry Cleaner, Inc.* v. *Stone, supra*
n. 56; *Nippert* v. *City of Richmond*, 327 U.S. 416, 425 (1946); *Best
& Co.* v. *Maxwell*, 311 U.S. 454, 455 ff. (1940).

[66] *Western Live Stock* v. *Bureau of Revenue*, 303 U.S. 250 (1938).
See generally Paul J. Hartman, *State Taxation of Interstate Commerce* (Buffalo, 1953), chs. 2, 3.

[67] E.g., *Freeman* v. *Hewit*, 329 U.S. 249, 263 (1946) (concurring
opinion).

It would be a hopeless task to embark on any discussion of the numerous forms of state taxes and the circumstances under which they have been declared valid or invalid. Exceedingly technical and complex rules have been developed with respect thereto, and generalization is both difficult and unsafe. But it should be a matter of especial interest that the Court, in determining the validity of a state tax, will today turn back to Marshall's decisions for guidance in its own. Thus, in the 1944 case of *Northwest Airlines* v. *Minnesota*,[68] Justice Jackson stated in a concurring opinion:

We are at a stage in development of air commerce roughly comparable to that of steamship navigation in 1824 when *Gibbons* v. *Ogden*, 9 Wheat. 1, come before this Court. Any authorization of local burdens on our national air commerce will lead to their multiplication in this country. Moreover, such an example is not likely to be neglected by other revenue-needy nations as international air transport expands. . . . The air is too precious as an open highway to permit it to be "owned" to the exclusion or embarrassment of air navigation by surface landlords who could put it to little real use.

Students of our legal evolution know how this Court interpreted the commerce clause of the Constitution to lift navigable waters of the United States out of local controls and into the domain of federal control. *Gibbons* v. *Ogden*, 9 Wheat. 1, to *United States* v. *Appalachian Power Co.*, 311 U.S. 377. Air as an element in which to navigate is even more inevitably federalized by the commerce clause than is navigable water. Local exactions and barriers to free transit in the air would neutralize its indifference to space and its conquest of time.[69]

The Northwest Airlines Case involved the validity of a Minnesota *ad valorem* property tax on all the planes of a

[68] 322 U.S. 292 (1944).   [69] *Ibid.*, pp. 302–303.

carrier domiciled in Minnesota but doing business on a regular basis in a number of other states as well.[70] Had the tax been a proportionate one, the problem would have been simpler;[71] but here there was the possibility that other states through which the planes passed might also impose a similar tax.[72] The effect of such other taxes was not considered in the majority opinion, and the Minnesota tax was sustained by a 5–4 vote. One of the concurring opinions expressed dissatisfaction with the "judicial formulation of general rules to meet the national problems arising from State taxation" bearing upon interstate commerce.[73] From the language used in the majority and in the concurring opinions, it is apparent that the Court was hospitable to the idea of a congressional solution of these problems.[74] In other words, may there not be situations in this area in which judicial solutions are inadequate because the total problems facing a particular industry reach the Court only by installments?[75] Suppose, for example, that a state imposes on an interstate carrier a tax based upon a formula for apportioning earnings within the state. But suppose that the carrier's net earnings are such that to meet the tax bill the carrier must draw upon earnings from other states. Obviously, if all the states in which the carrier operates exacted a tax similarly computed, the carrier would be forced into bankruptcy; if only some of those states exacted such a tax, the carrier's total earnings

[70] *Ibid.*, pp. 293–294.
[71] See the language of Justice Jackson in his concurring opinion, *ibid.*, pp. 305–307.
[72] *Ibid.*, pp. 305–306.   [73] *Ibid.*, p. 302.
[74] *Ibid.*, pp. 300, 302, 306. See also *McCarroll* v. *Dixie Greyhound Lines, Inc.*, 309 U.S. 176, 185, 188 (1939) (dissenting opinion).
[75] Cf. *Northwest Airlines* v. *U.S., supra* n. 68, at 307.

would be severely depressed. Would the Court strike down such a tax as an undue burden on interstate commerce, or would an act of Congress be first required? [76] If the Court was unwilling, as it was in the Northwest Airlines Case, to consider the effect of possible taxation by other states, on the ground that such possible taxes were not before the Court, the latter solution would seem to be the only alternative.[77] The old principles and doctrines may prove too difficult to apply to new problems, or at least to be embarrassing in their effects. The commerce clause, in other words, may prove to have limitations which even Marshall could not foresee.

One thing seems plain from a reading of recent Supreme Court decisions, and that is a growing recognition on the part of the Court that questions involving the power of Congress under the commerce clause cannot be decided by reference to mechanical tests or to such formulae as "direct" and "indirect" burdens upon commerce. This change is illustrated by the tax cases as well as by the regulatory cases. Thirteen years ago, Justice Jackson re-

[76] See the concurring opinion of Justice Black, *ibid.*, p. 302: "Until it [Congress] acts I think we should enter the field with extreme caution."

[77] It is not entirely clear how far Congress could go in relieving an interstate carrier from the burdens of state taxation. In his concurring opinion in the Northwest Airlines Case, *supra* n. 68, pp. 303–304, Justice Jackson said: "Congress has not extended its protection and control to the field of taxation, although I take it no one denies that constitutionally it may do so. It may exact a single uniform federal tax on the property or business to the exclusion of taxation by the states. It may subject the vehicles or other incidents to any type of state and local taxation, or *it may declare them tax-free altogether*" (emphasis supplied). It seems open to question whether an act of Congress forbidding all state taxation of interstate carriers might not be thought to exceed its power and hence not find judicial sanction.

ferred with approval to the new line of cases which invoked "broader interpretations of the Commerce Clause destined to . . . bring about a return to the principles first enunciated by Chief Justice Marshall in *Gibbons* v. *Ogden*." [78] It is fair to conclude, therefore, that Marshall's commerce-clause decisions have a continuing significance not only for solving the problems of state regulations of commerce, but also—and particularly in this century, from the standpoint of the broad purposes of the commerce clause—for defining the scope and extent of federal power in terms of a unified and integrated national economic structure. Chief Justice Stone once set forth the paramount importance of the commerce clause in these words: [79]

Great as is the practical wisdom exhibited in all the provisions of the Constitution, . . . it will, I believe, be the judgment of history that the Commerce Clause and the wise interpretation of it, perhaps more than any other contributing element, have united to bind the several states into a nation.

This continuing influence of three cases decided more than 130 years ago is in large part the result of a great quality that Marshall possessed, a quality particularly exemplified in his great decisions involving the commerce clause. *Gibbons* v. *Ogden* illustrates with especial force the truth of the statement of William Draper Lewis, that the lasting character of Marshall's work lay not in the fact that it was the work of a statesman but the work of a judge.[80] Had he been merely a far-sighted statesman, his

[78] *Wickard* v. *Filburn, supra* n. 54, p. 122.
[79] Harlan F. Stone, "Fifty Years' Work of the United States Supreme Court," *Am. Bar Assn. Journal*, XIV (1928), 428, 430.
[80] William D. Lewis, "John Marshall," in *Great American Lawyers*, ed. by W. D. Lewis (Philadelphia, 1907–1909), II, 372.

cases would undoubtedly have been decided in the same way. What has made them endure is the fact that they were the work of a lawyer to whom the ground for every premise had to be carefully prepared, every possible objection examined and answered, every conclusion clearly and concisely stated.[81] The completeness of analysis, the wealth of illustration, gives the reader the conviction that the subject has not only been adequately treated but exhausted.[82] His power of phrase was such that today, when lawyers and judges wish to express the constitutional principles he enunciated, they revert to his own choice of words. Unpopular as most of his opinions were, Marshall's contemporary influence was immense, and he affected profoundly the political as well as the legal thinking of the bar. Because so many politicians of his day were lawyers, this means also that he affected to a substantial degree the political thinking of people at large. Professor Corwin has referred to the curious infusion of politics and jurisprudence which has so characterized the course of discussion and legislation in America, and he has remarked that no public career in American history ever built so largely upon that pervasive trait of the national outlook as did Marshall's.[83] But it is submitted that his influence became all-pervasive because his opinions—carefully reasoned, lawyerlike opinions—were studied generation after generation by law students, by practitioners, and by judges, and his opinions, therefore, live almost as if they were a part of the Constitution itself.

[81] *Ibid.*, p. 375.   [82] *Ibid.*
[83] Edward S. Corwin, *John Marshall and the Constitution* (New Haven, 1919), p. 197.

X. Marshall, the Marshall

Court, and the Constitution

BY DONALD G. MORGAN

ONE prerequisite of a proper appraisal of John Marshall's contribution to the law, and particularly to the law of the Constitution, would seem to be the balancing of the roles played by Marshall himself and by the Court over which he presided. In preparing a life of Marshall's long-time associate, William Johnson, the author has been increasingly impressed by this need. Even the reasonably well-informed student assumes that Marshall completely dominated his brothers, that the leading constitutional pronouncements of that period were almost exclusively Marshall's in conception as well as expression, that those shadowy figures who flanked him on the supreme bench were effectual only insofar as they nodded their approval of his decrees—in short, that Marshall was the Court.

Such a conception pictures the great Chief Justice as possessing to a superhuman degree a prophetic judgment

The Marshall Court

and a persuasive manner. That such a conception exists results both from the tributes of his supporters, early and late, and from the charges of his antagonists; Jefferson, himself, complained to a host of friends of the subtle skill by which a "crafty chief judge" reduced to silent acquiescence his "lazy or timid associates."

Yet to advance such a conception is to do no service to Marshall. As Justice Frankfurter has written: "Marshall himself, hardheaded as he was and free from obvious self-deception, would doubtless be greatly amused by the claim that he was the whole of his Court." [1]

The author believes that Marshall's influence was not the same as commonly supposed. That the Court was more than Marshall is the lesson of weighty considerations. For one thing, Marshall was but one of six, and, after 1807, one of seven members of the Court. Whatever may have been his qualities of mind and character, and these were notable, that was his actual voting strength. Like the British Prime Minister, he was, in relation to his brothers, only *primus inter pares*.

Consider, moreover, those fifteen associate justices who sat, at one time or another, on the Marshall Court. Out of fifteen, one might expect to find some with spirit and convictions. There were on the Court men with maturity and experience. Observe that nine of the fifteen had served in their state legislatures, and six in Congress; five had served in state and an equal number in federal administrative posts; no fewer than eleven had had previous judicial experience. [2]

[1] Felix Frankfurter, *The Commerce Clause* (Chapel Hill, N.C., 1937), p. 5.
[2] Figures adapted from Cortez A. M. Ewing, *Judges of the Supreme Court, 1789–1937* (Minneapolis, Minn., 1938).

Furthermore, although Marshall held tenaciously to a definite constitutional theory, he was far from doctrinaire in pursuing it. With equal earnestness he also sought a united and harmonious Court; for as Justice Johnson explained to Jefferson, Marshall deplored the "indecency of judges cutting at each other" and "the loss of reputation" which such a practice might engender. When Johnson arrived on the Court, he found Marshall giving all the opinions in decisions in which he partook "even in some instances when contrary to his own judgment and vote." [3] It is clear that Marshall sought to maintain a nice balance between his two overriding objectives—expounding officially his basic Federalist constitutional theory and maintaining a solid judicial front as a means of enhancing the authoritativeness of the Court.

Finally, other forces besides Marshall's persuasiveness beat on the judges during those years. Events such as the War of 1812 and movements such as the revival of states' rights sentiments in the 1820's must have had their effect and helped shape the direction of adjudications. In short, the Court was neither static nor isolated from the common public destiny.

This, therefore, was a collegial body, and one that would respond to change within as well as to change without. On this assumption, therefore, this paper seeks to explore the contributions of Marshall himself and of the Court as a collectivity. A study of the record of unity and division, and of Marshall's relations with his colleagues, will, it is hoped, make possible a more accurate appraisal of Marshall's influence both in extent and character.

[3] Johnson to Jefferson, Dec. 10, 1822, Jefferson Papers MS, Library of Congress; see also *Little* v. *Barreme*, 2 Cranch 170, 179 (1804).

To this end, it is the intention here to examine the work of the Court during five successive periods. The periods have been determined by changes in Court personnel. For each period the composition and practices of the Court will be briefly considered; and in each instance the positions taken by the Court on three major questions of constitutional interpretation will be analyzed: first, national powers, that is, the breadth of discretion assigned to the federal government and its capacity to carry its enactments into execution through its own instrumentalities; second, state powers, as affected both by powers assigned to the federal government and by express constitutional prohibitions; third, the separation of powers, especially as it affects the relative positions of Congress and the judiciary. Most of the leading constitutional questions which arose at that time can be comprehended within these three categories. This study of the changing attitudes of the changing Court may furnish clues to the true character of the Marshall Court and of Marshall's influence.

I

In the period 1801–1804 there was Federalist unanimity on the Court. Beside the newly arrived Marshall sat William Cushing, William Paterson, Samuel Chase, Bushrod Washington, and Alfred Moore. In the face of Jefferson's hostile administration, the judges drew together and gave the impression of impeccable unity. No dissent was rendered, and but one separate concurring opinion; Marshall spoke for the Court in every case over which he presided. Disagreements were suppressed in the effort to create a united front.

Chief Justice John Marshall

In this period no very significant pronouncements were made concerning either national powers or state powers. Two decisions did, however, affect the relations between the Court and Congress. Despite uncertainties among the judges, the Court, in *Stuart* v. *Laird,* acceded to wide congressional control over inferior federal courts. Yet, in *Marbury* v. *Madison,* the Court declared through Marshall that the President is accountable to the law for his acts; that Article III, by specifying the Court's original jurisdiction, strictly limits Congress; and, most significantly, that the Court may judge the constitutionality of acts of Congress. The Marbury Case set the tone for the period. By relinquishing jurisdiction over this mandamus, the Court asserted an undefined authority to construe the limits of the constitutional powers of Congress.

II

Nominally, at least, the years 1805–1811 were a period of Republican minority. William Johnson of South Carolina appeared in Washington in 1805 to take the place of Moore; Henry Brockholst Livingston of New York replaced Paterson in 1807, and Thomas Todd of Kentucky appeared in 1808 to occupy a new seventh seat on the Court. Yet the Republicans were at times more than a minority, since the enfeebled Chase and Cushing took only a sporadic part in the Court's work, although both remained long enough to give James Madison rather than Jefferson the opportunity of appointing their successors.

A careful reading of the reports, supplemented by the testimony of Johnson, shows that a good deal of experimentation took place in the procedure for the rendering of opinions. In several early decisions opinions were given seriatim, that is, separately by all the judges. Occasionally individual judges, differing from the majority, delivered their own dissenting or concurring opinions. Yet the dominant mode was the single opinion, written by the Chief Justice. When the Court divided, the size of the majority and the identity of the dissenters often remained a mystery, a condition that led to confusion both for contemporaries and for later scholars.

In this period, issues of national power began to appear in the Court. In a case concerning bankruptcy in 1805, the Court, with little fanfare, went a long way toward upholding implied powers in Congress, and this with the approval of Jefferson's new appointee, William Johnson. Four years later, an ostensibly unanimous Court, now including three Republicans, repudiated an effort by Pennsylvania to interfere with the enforcement of decrees by the federal district court. In cases involving state power, however, the seeds of later divisions were planted. In one of his first decisions, Johnson publicly took issue with Marshall and the majority on the deference due to state legislative enactments concerning land titles.[4] And in the great case of *Fletcher* v. *Peck* in 1810 in which the Court, through Marshall, voided the Georgia land grant repealer on the twin grounds of natural law and the contract clause of the Constitution, Johnson spoke out again. He questioned not only the bona fide character of the controversy, but also the applicability of the contract clause to it. His appeal to natural law saved this from being an open dissent, but the soil was prepared for later cleavages.

[4] The former cases were *U.S.* v. *Fisher* (1805) and *U.S.* v. *Peters* (1809); the latter case was *Huidekoper's Lessee* v. *Douglass* (1805).

Chief Justice John Marshall

On the relative positions of Congress and the judiciary, few important adjudications were made. In two instances, Johnson diverged from Marshall on the character of Congress' control of court jurisdiction. The majority tended to interpret jurisdictional clauses broadly, and Johnson, narrowly.[5]

Thus the departure of Federalists from the Court during this period encouraged not only open divisions but divergences in two of the three areas of constitutional interpretation.

III

For several reasons the third period, from 1812 to 1823, was easily the most notable. President Madison in 1811 chose Joseph Story of Massachusetts and Gabriel Duvall of Maryland to occupy the places of Chase and Cushing. Thereupon, the Court was constituted as follows: two Federalists, Marshall and Washington, both Adams' appointees; three Jeffersonians, Johnson, Livingston, and Todd; and the two new Madison men. Beginning in 1812, these seven continued to meet for twelve successive terms. This is by far the longest period without personnel change in the Court's entire history. Furthermore, the questions confronting the judges became increasingly important. They went to the heart of the constitutional system.

In this period the Court at last settled down to a regular mode of opinion-giving. This mode, in Johnson's words, was "to appoint someone to deliver the opinion of the

[5] *Ex parte* Bollman (1807) and *Bank of the United States* v. *Deveaux* (1809), as commented on by Johnson in *Bank of the United States* v. *Planters' Bank of Georgia* (1824).

majority, but leave it to the discretion of the rest of the judges to record their opinions or not ad libitum." [6] A single majority opinion would make for authoritativeness; the recognition of a right of independent-minded judges to speak for themselves would protect free expression. Notable exceptions, of course, were the great cases of 1819 and 1821, which for the most part were unanimous. Yet differences did exist and frequently came to the surface during this all-important middle third of Marshall's tenure.

As in the preceding period, the greatest degree of unanimity appeared in controversies concerning questions of national power. In wartime cases involving ship seizures and delegations of power to the President, in a case defending national power over naturalization, in the great Bank Case establishing firmly the doctrine of implied congressional power and the tax immunity of federal instrumentalities, in the pivotal decision supporting a congressional contempt power, and in the decision which fixed firmly the appellate jurisdiction of the Supreme Court over state judiciaries—in all of these the Court spoke firmly, emphatically, and unanimously.[7] Indeed the unity seemed to deepen with the passage of time.

Contrast this solid unity on issues of national power with the tentative explorations and divergences in relation to state powers. Note the groping toward a sound and practicable way of construing state powers that shade into federal powers. Simply put, the question was whether the granting of a power to the national government *ipso facto*

[6] Letter cited in note 2 above.
[7] See the *Rapid* (1814), the *Aurora* (1813), *Chirac v. Chirac* (1817), *McCulloch v. Maryland* (1819), *Anderson v. Dunn* (1821), *Cohens v. Virginia* (1821).

175

had withdrawn that power from the states, or whether the states, in the absence of contradictory congressional legislation, might exercise a concurrent power in the field. A careful study of *Martin* v. *Hunter* (1816), *Sturges* v. *Crowninshield* (1819), and *Houston* v. *Moore* (1820), reveals the Court sharply divided on the issue; Justices Story and Washington tended to support exclusive power, and Johnson, with the probable adherence of others, favored concurrent power. Marshall, although tending to favor exclusive power, appears to have approached the problem somewhat empirically, with the aim either of mediating the differences or of seeking from the opposed doctrines the best and most practicable constructions for each case.

Another line of cases concerning state powers found the Court again divided, although here less ostensibly. In a series of rulings under that clause which prohibits states from passing laws "impairing the obligation of contracts," the Court struck down state laws. The majority steadily expanded the scope of the clause, thus protecting from subsequent state regulation a tax-exemption feature of a land grant (1812), a college charter (1819), a private contract (1819), and a land title under an interstate compact (1823).[8]

The reports of these cases show that in almost every instance the Court stood divided on the point in question. Yet in all but the last case, in 1823, the minority kept silent; and that fact made all the more abrupt the subsequent shift in the trend of decisions.

The separation of powers now came into adjudication less frequently than before. In 1812 the majority, over the

[8] *New Jersey* v. *Wilson, Dartmouth College* v. *Woodward, Sturges* v. *Crowninshield*, and *Green* v. *Biddle*.

silent opposition of Story, and probably Marshall among others, had rejected a jurisdiction to try crimes at the common law and insisted on congressional control of federal criminal jurisdiction.[9] In effect, this action benefited the state judiciaries as well as Congress. Again, one wing of the Court felt that in many instances Congress, not the Court, should determine whether states under their concurrent powers might deal with subjects already partially touched on by Congress.

This, then, was most truly the Marshall Court. The judges stood together in upholding broad national powers and the means of carrying into execution such powers. Even here, however, the hand of a minority may be detected, as in the McCulloch Case, where Marshall felt constrained to delimit the scope of the ruling on state taxation, a condition which he brushed aside a few years later.[10] Elsewhere, the evidence of division is clear. Divergences were pronounced, and the Court felt its way toward satisfactory solutions. The opposition, however, never crystallized, never organized into a permanent bloc. Its components, though probably numbering Johnson, sometimes Livingston, occasionally Todd or Duvall, shifted with the issue. It was not only a loyal opposition, it was an unorganized opposition. That it remained so was unquestionably the result of Marshall's tact and generalship.

IV

The period from 1824 to 1829 was essentially one of transition. In meeting controversies, the Court at times

[9] *U.S.* v. *Hudson and Goodwin.*
[10] See 4 Wheat. 436 and *Weston* v. *Charleston* (1829).

seemed to hesitate and then to alter its course. Out of the climate of public criticism over its antistate and self-assertive policies came two new appointees, Smith Thompson of New York, in the place of Livingston in 1824, and Robert Trimble of Kentucky, in the place of Todd in 1827.

In response to attacks on the Court, Marshall, Story, and Duvall now drew together in agreement both on principle and on the need of Court unanimity; henceforth, with rare exceptions, the three acted and spoke as one. Oddly enough, Washington, the lone Federalist among the associate justices, on one notable occasion diverged from them; conceivably it was he who wielded the balance of power, at least after Todd's departure. The other judges showed signs of revolt. In 1824 Johnson announced in the Gibbons Case his determination to speak his mind in constitutional cases, a resolve to which he adhered. Thompson more than once dissented from the dominant opinion. The short-lived Trimble remained only long enough to show his affinity with these last two on at least some issues.

What would be Marshall's policy whenever the minority should threaten to become the majority? Would he dissent in behalf of a favored doctrine and thus cause a break in the Court's solid front, or would he remain the spokesman of a united Court in support of interpretations which he personally deprecated? Here was a major challenge to his generalship.

Once again the problem of national powers found the Court in solid agreement. In *Gibbons* v. *Ogden*, the Steamboat Case, the Court depicted the power to regulate commerce in the broadest terms; in *Martin* v. *Mott* it endorsed broad national control over the militia. In *Ameri-*

can Insurance Co. v. *Canter* it resolved Jefferson's earlier dilemma by upholding a broad power to acquire and govern territories, here against the claims of the judicial article.

In another leading case, *Osborn* v. *Bank*, it declared the lower federal courts open to the national bank for injunction protection from hostile state measures.[11]

But now long-smoldering disputes over state powers broke into flame.[12] Should the interest which a citizen received on federal bank securities be immune from a state income tax? The Court split sharply over this issue in *Weston* v. *Charleston* in 1829. For the majority, the Chief Justice found no discrimination in the tax, but nevertheless held it invalid as a potential burden on the federal power to borrow. The ruling went a long step beyond the McCulloch decision against the Maryland tax on the Bank's note issue. Johnson and Thompson sharply dissented; Johnson, as elsewhere, objected to the assumption that the states were essentially hostile to federal measures and agencies.

The most thorough break with the past came in *Ogden* v. *Saunders* in 1827. Again, the Court was considering a state law for the relief of insolvent debtors, this time as applied to debts contracted after its passage. Four of the seven judges—Washington, Johnson, Thompson and Trimble—supported the law. So convinced was Marshall in his

[11] Johnson dissented on the matter of jurisdiction, but used this occasion to defend the establishment of the Bank as an exertion of broad fiscal powers.

[12] In the Gibbons Case, both Marshall and Johnson explored the relationship between state powers and the federal commerce power; although the former tentatively, and the latter conclusively, endorsed exclusive power in Congress, both opened a broad area for the operation of the state police powers as they might affect commerce. Marshall here retained his somewhat tentative approach to exclusive powers.

conservatism, that on this occasion he delivered, with the acquiescence of Story and Duvall, a powerful dissenting opinion. The majority judges had weakened the impact of their decision by speaking separately, a fact which may well have encouraged Marshall to press hard his minority views.

Marshall's opinion was a logical extension of the earlier rulings; had it prevailed, it would have further tightened the hold of the contract clause on economic regulations by states. But the majority, following Johnson's pioneering opinion in *Green* v. *Biddle* in 1823, shifted the direction of the decision and thus enabled the states to meet substantial economic needs of their inhabitants.

No serious clashes between the pretensions of Congress and those of the Court occurred in this period. Yet, here, as in the cases on state powers, one detects a divergence in philosophy. The Ogden and other cases suggest that the Marshall wing, distrusting popular rule and seeking narrowly to confine state legislatures in their efforts at regulation, regarded it as the high duty of the Court to put down measures that seemed to them arbitrary; the Court, in short, was to be the policeman of the federal system. Other judges, however, were tending to pursue a policy of judicial restraint, to leave a broader discretion for states in their internal measures, and to look to Congress for guidance, where federal power converged on state powers. Again, however, the minority usually remained a minority and never coalesced into a bloc.

V

The arrival in 1830 of two appointees of Andrew Jackson set the stage for a new era. The tide was now flowing toward the support of state regulations and toward judicial noninterference. For Trimble, John McLean of Ohio, and for Washington, Henry Baldwin of Pennsylvania, came as replacements; Johnson died in 1834, and James M. Wayne of Georgia took his place at Marshall's final term. The new arrivals signaled their appearance by upsetting the arrangements for common living quarters, by questioning dominant lines of interpretation, and by swelling dramatically the volume of dissent. Dissenting opinions, which had recently averaged in number slightly more than two a year, now leaped to ten in 1830, seven in 1831, and eight in 1832. With Washington now gone, Marshall faced a formidable challenge, for on many issues the new men stood with Johnson and Thompson.

On national powers, no serious issues arose. Earlier precedents were now so firmly fixed that the justices would have been hard put to it to explain departures with any consistency. Nor was there, one may suppose, any zest for challenging those precedents when Georgia and South Carolina were in open defiance of federal power.

But state powers were a different matter. Most of the cases in this category involved the meaning of express constitutional prohibitions, of which three may be cited. First, the contract clause was again argued as a defense against state regulations. Now the Court seemed anxious to repudiate implications that might have been drawn from the early decisions. Significantly, it was not Marshall, but Johnson, who spoke for the Court in *Hawkins* v. *Barney* (1831), which strongly defended state limitation statutes, and in *Livingston* v. *Moore* (1833), which maintained the power of the state to provide and adjust remedies for enforcing contracts. Marshall, himself, in the Providence Bank Case (1830), spoke favorably of the state's tax power and refused to discover in a bank charter any implied exemption from taxation. In all of this it was an ostensibly unanimous Court that undercut the spirit, if not the letter, of earlier adjudications.

Second, the prohibition against bills of credit was argued as a bar to the Missouri loan office certificates in the Craig Case. Here a bare majority invalidated the state law, but a trio of dissenters, Johnson, Thompson, and McLean, spoke up for the state.

Again, when John Barron appealed to the Fifth Amendment in contending that Baltimore had, through harbor improvements, taken his wharf properties without just compensation, the Court read the Bill of Rights as limiting only the federal government. Again, the spirit of the decision departed from that of a decade earlier.

The question of the separation of powers seldom came into litigation.[13] In general, the current was running strongly in favor of legislative power as an instrument for social action.

One is mystified by Marshall's role in many of the cases of this period. There is little doubt that he retained his earlier convictions about the judicial function and the threat latent in state powers. Yet he was now expressing, or acquiescing in, statements challenging those convictions at several points. In his quest for a firm and united Court

[13] In the Cherokee Nation Case in 1831, the Court refused to decide a suit brought by the tribe against Georgia; yet a year later, in the Worcester Case, it accepted the appeal of a private citizen and provoked President Jackson's defiance by deciding against the state and inferentially calling for enforcement by the executive. The two decisions, in both of which the Court stood divided, show the tribunal uncertain and somewhat hesitant to thrust itself into such controversies.

it is wholly conceivable that in the leading cases, such as Providence Bank, he chose to formulate the opinion in his own terms and that in others, such as the Hawkins Case, he left their formulation to an ancient and trusted colleague. By this period, also, one must allow for declining strength in a man now in his late seventies and admire the hold he was still able to maintain over a Court that without him would doubtless have split into fragments.

VI

From the foregoing analysis it is possible to draw several conclusions: (1) The passing of final judgment on the inner workings of the Marshall Court awaits the completion of special studies of individual judges. Particularly desirable is a good modern biography of Joseph Story. Of value also would be shorter studies of such justices as Bushrod Washington, Henry Brockholst Livingston, and Smith Thompson.

(2) The judges stood solidly together on some constitutional issues and divided on others. Where the power of the national government and its capacity to effectuate its policies were concerned, disagreement was rare. The striking unanimity that prevailed here suggests that Marshall's pronational convictions may have had some effect. One may, however, find additional motives for this degree of unity in the necessities of federation, the pressure of events, and the inclination, noted even in Jefferson himself, of those holding federal office to perceive and to supply the power needs of the central government.

On state power the record shows mounting disagreement. If Marshall may privately have favored exclusive powers in the federal government, he publicly followed a policy of empiricism which enabled him to endorse the trend toward concurrent state power. He evidently had his way in contract-clause cases until 1827; his failure in the Ogden Case, however, proves that the other judges had minds of their own and the power to reject his leadership. It suggests that thereafter Marshall may have pressed his convictions only as far as a majority would follow him.

Questions of the judicial function likewise produced divisions. The prevailing trend was toward judicial restraint in favor of legislative action, state and federal. Doubtless this formed a part of the popular trend toward democracy, and Marshall, despite his personal inclinations, went along with the tide.

(3) The constitutional interpretation that characterized the years 1801–1835 was the work not of Marshall, but of the Marshall Court. Many judges contributed to the final result. In Justice Frankfurter's words, the behavior of the Court was an "orchestral, and not a solo performance." [14]

(4) The identity of the orchestra's director, however, was never in doubt. Marshall sought harmony as much as he sought to propagate his own views. Like the good team captain, he kept the peace within the ranks, listened to protests, and at times allowed others to share the lime-light.

The absence of an embittered minority bloc is evidence of his success. William Johnson, indeed, might have headed such a bloc. In learning, wisdom, and firmness of character, Johnson had few peers on the early Court. But Johnson lacked precisely those qualities of personality and temperament that so well equipped Marshall for his task.

[14] *Commerce Clause*, p. 43.

(5) To a great degree, the measure of Marshall's influence, therefore, was in his qualities of character and personal leadership. The eminence acquired by the Supreme Court during that period and the strength imparted to the Constitution are less the work of Marshall the convinced Federalist than of Marshall the man. Here was a statesman, not a zealot; an empiricist, not a dogmatist; a leader, not a tyrant.

—

Note on the Contributors

IRVING BRANT. Editor, Writer. Washington, D.C., Author of *Storm over the Constitution* (1936) and *James Madison* (1941–1953).

JOSEPH DORFMAN. Professor of Economics, Columbia University. Author of *Thorstein Veblen and His America* (1934) and *The Economic Mind in American Civilization* (1946–49).

CHARLES FAIRMAN. Professor of Law, Harvard University. Author of *The Law of Martial Rule* (1930) and *Justice Miller and the Supreme Court, 1862–1890* (1939).

JULIUS GOEBEL, Jr. Professor of Law, Columbia University. Author of *The Recognition Policy of the United States* (1915), *The Equality of States* (1923), and *Law Enforcement in Colonial New York* (1944) with T. Raymond Naughton.

GEORGE L. HASKINS. Professor of Law, University of Pennsylvania. Author of *Statute of York and the Interest of the Commons* (1935) and *The Growth of English Representative Government* (1948).

Chief Justice John Marshall

ARTHUR N. HOLCOMBE. Professor of Government, Emeritus, Harvard University. Author of *Human Rights in the Modern World* (1948) and *Our More Perfect Union* (1950).

DAVID J. MAYS. Attorney, Richmond, Virginia. Author of *Business Law* (1933) and *Edmund Pendleton, 1721–1803* (1952).

DONALD G. MORGAN. Professor of Political Science, Mt. Holyoke College. Author of *Justice Johnson, the First Dissenter* (1954).

F. D. G. RIBBLE. Dean of the Law School, University of Virginia. Author of *State and National Power over Commerce* (1937).

CARL BRENT SWISHER. Professor of Political Science, Johns Hopkins University. Author of *Roger B. Taney* (1936), *American Constitutional Development* (1943), and *Theory and Practice of American National Government* (1951).

Index

189

Index

191

Index

Index

Missouri v. Holland, 82
Monroe, James, 30, 35, 56
Montesquieu, Spirit of Laws, 126
Moore, Alfred, 171
Morris, Gouverneur, 34
Morris, Robert, 44
Murdock & Co. v. Hunter, 119 n. 39

Nankin v. Chander, 120 n. 40
National Bankruptcy Act, 126
National defense, constitution and, 86
National Labor Relations Board v. Jones and Laughlin, 72
National Motor Vehicle Theft Act, 158
NATO, 92
Neutrality Proclamation, Marshall on, 29
New Jersey v. Wilson, 176 n. 8
New York v. Miln, 98
New York v. U.S., 69
Nicholas, Wilson Cary, 41
Nippert v. City of Richmond, 162
Northwest Airlines v. Minnesota, 163

Ogden v. Saunders, 131, 179
Osborn v. Bank of the United States, 58, 96, 179

Paper money, opposed by Marshall, 137
Parsons' Cause, and judicial review, 20
Paterson, William, Justice, 78, 171
Pendleton, Edmund, Judge, 21, 54, 111
Penhallow v. Doane's Admins., 112 n. 20
Pickering, Timothy, 45
Pickett v. Morris, 111 n. 17
Pinckney, Charles Cotesworth, 56
Pinkney, William, 54, 59
Plumer, William, Senator, 50
Police powers
  of national government, 158
  of states, 72, 130, 155

Political parties, Marshall on, 31
Presidency, independence of supported by Marshall, 32, 47
Price control, Marshall on, 138, 139
Prize law, Marshall on, 92
Process Act of 1789, 105
Process Act of 1792, 105 n. 7
Property rights, Marshall on, 9, 131
Providence Bank v. Billings, 136, 181, 183
Public debt, Marshall on, 138
Pure Food and Drug Act, 158

Quarantine laws, under state control, 139, 149
Quincy, Josiah, 56

Randolph, Edmund, 54
Randolph, John, 22, 50, 150 n. 28
Reconstruction Acts, judicial review passes, 67
Religion, established, Marshall on, 27
Remonstrance, the, in Virginia, 22
Rhinelander v. Insurance Company of Pa., 127
Ritchie, Editor, 59
Roane, Spencer, 54, 59, 78, 79
Robinson v. Campbell, 122
Rodney, Caesar, 52
Roman law, 80
Ross v. Poythress, 111 n. 18
Roy v. Garnett, 111 n. 17

Schooner Exchange v. McFaddon, 92
Seaboard Air Line Railway v. Blackwell, 157
Sedgwick, Theodore, 30, 45
Seldon v. Hendrickson, 136
Sherman Anti-Trust Act, 71, 158
Shermer v. Shermer's Executors, 111 n. 17
Short v. Skipwith, 120 n. 40
Slavery, Marshall on, 26
Smith, Adam, and Marshall, 128
Smith, Robert, 57
South Carolina v. U.S., 69

193

Index

Index